The UNKNOWING SAGE

The Life and Work of Baba Faqir Chand

ईमानदारी

The
UNKNOWING
SAGE

The Life and Work of Baba Faqir Chand

ईमानदारी

Mt. San Antonio College
Walnut, California

Fifth Edition: 2014

ISBN: 978-1-56543-254-3

MSAC Philosophy Group
Mt. San Antonio College
1100 Walnut, California 91789 USA

Website: http://www.neuralsurfer.com

Imprint: *The Runnebohm Library Series*

Publication History: This book was first published in the United States in 1981. A series of subsequent editions followed over the next three decades. Faqir Chand personally dictated his autobiography in Urdu at the express request of David Lane and it was then translated into English by Professor Bhagat Ram Kamal, who is now the spiritual head of Manavta Mandir.

The
UNKNOWING
SAGE

The Life and Work of Baba Faqir Chand

ईमानदारी

Mt. San Antonio College
Walnut, California

Fifth Edition: 2014

ISBN: 978-1-56543-254-3

MSAC Philosophy Group
Mt. San Antonio College
1100 Walnut, California 91789 USA

Website: http://www.neuralsurfer.com

Imprint: *The Runnebohm Library Series*

Publication History: This book was first published in the United States in 1981. A series of subsequent editions followed over the next three decades. Faqir Chand personally dictated his autobiography in Urdu at the express request of David Lane and it was then translated into English by Professor Bhagat Ram Kamal, who is now the spiritual head of Manavta Mandir.

Dedication

To Professor Bhagat Ram Kamal

I have had the unique privilege of knowing Professor Bhagat Ram Kamal since the summer of 1978 when we first met at Manavta Mandir where Professor Kamal served as my personal liason with Baba Faqir Chand. He was instrumental in publishing my first interview of Faqir (alongwith Professor Juergensmeyer's) back in 1978 under the title "The Master Speaks to the Foreigners." Professor Kamal knows the life and teachings of Baba Faqir Chand better than anyone currently living and has a unique insight into Faqir's radical and uncompromising philosophy. This work would not be possible without Professor Kamal's keen intelligence and guiding hand.

धन्यवाद

Table of Contents

The Faqir Chand Library Series

On Faqir Chand [1886 to 1981] was a remarkable Indian sage who spent over seventy-five years practicing an ancient meditation technique, popularly known today as surat shabd yoga, which attempts to induce a consciously controlled near-death experience. Mastery of this practice, according to adepts of the tradition, enables one to experience regions of light and sound beyond the normal waking state, providing glimpses into higher realms of consciousness. After the end of World War One, Faqir Chand was recognized by his own guru Shiv Brat Lal and others in the movement to be an advanced shabd yoga mystic. According to Faqir's own account, he could almost daily leave his body at will and experience exalted states of awareness. Nevertheless, Faqir Chand was not satisfied with these attainments and sought for something higher and more, permanent Eventually Faqir realized that no matter how subtle or blissful a meditation experience may be, it did not in and of itself constitutes the ultimate in spiritual realization. Rather, the ultimate truth was that no experience could capture or contain the transcendental mystery of Being. In the highest stages of development man does not develop a keen sense of omniscience, but a radical and irrevocable understanding of unknowingness. In sum, one realizes that he or she is nothing but a mere bubble in a sea of existence that is infinite in all directions. As such, the bubble simply surrenders its entire being to that Power which is, in truth, living it.

Thus Faqir Chand became quite outspoken about how gurus, masters, prophets, and mystics, posing as all-knowing beings, have deceived millions of followers by duping them into believing that they have omnipresence and omnipotence when in fact they have neither. What enlightened sages possess, rather, is access experientially to a higher spectrum of awareness, which, in tum, reveals not final or absolute truth, but a growing awareness of how truly mysterious life really is. As Shiv Dayal Singh, the founder of Radhasoami, poetically put it: "Wonder, Wonder, Wonder; Wonder hath assumed a form." Coupled with Faqir's tacit realization of unknowingness, he also exposed for the first time in the Sant *tradition* how visions of religious personages are the products of one's own inner development.

For instance, when one undergoes a near- death experience and beholds a Jesus or a Nanak or an Angel in the middle of the light at the end of a long, dark tunnel, it is not the esteemed figure who is himself orchestrating the encounter. Rather it is the neophyte who is projecting the sacred personage on to the light from his/her own biological and cultural history. The light may well indeed be a transcultural phenomenon, part and parcel of a higher order of awareness or merely a neurological event, but the interpretation of who resides in that light (Is it Jesus? Is it Nanak? Is it my uncle Joe?) is entirely a personal affair, shaded by the nuances of an individual's sojourn for tens of years on a planet we call Earth.

Faqir is perhaps best known for his frank admissions of ignorance surrounding his miraculous appearances to disciples during times of need. He unilaterally confessed that he was never aware of appearing to his devotees. Nor did Faqir Chand claim that h had understood the secret of Reality. As he said on many occasions, echoing the words of such greats as Lao Tzu, Socrates, and Nicholas of Cusa: " How can I make any claims about attaining the Ultimate. The truth is that I know nothing." Hence, Faqir Chand raised the slogan of "Be-Man," arguing that to become a human being, endowed with discrimination and compassion, is a great thing in itself. To be spiritual, Faqir would assert, necessitates that one become a true man (or woman) first. The Mt San Antonio Philosophy Group, while not advocating any one position in philosophy or religion, established the Faqir Chand Library Series in honor of *vichar*, "clear thinking." As the late Sardar Bahadur Jagat Singh, a contemporary of Faqir's, once stated, "Clear thinking is 90% of spirituality." Future volumes in the series will include works in both science and religion that promote the Chandian spirit of honest and frank criticism. This volume, *The Unknowing Sage*, represents the first comprehensive study of Baba Faqir Chand's life and work in English.

A Note to the Reader

On September 11, 1981, Baba Faqir Chand, the renowned master of surat shabd yoga, died. He was ninety-five years old. Although the public at large remained unaware of this event, there were a small number of sages, yogis, and mystics in India, Europe, and North America who realized that humanity had lost one of the great sages to appear in this century. Having known Baba Faqir Chand personally and being aware of his failing condition, I wrote to him in the summer of 1980 at his ashram in Hoshiarpur (near the Himalayan foothills) asking if he would write his life story before he left the world. To the joy of myself and other interested scholars and seekers, Faqir kindly accepted the request with the following blessing: "You can do this work. I will help you with the experiences of my life. I heartily wish you success in your life in all aspects. My love and respect to you."

Baba Faqir Chand subsequently dictated his autobiography in Urdu and had it translated for me into English. What Faqir has presented both in his life narrative and numerous spiritual treatises is without precedent in the Sant Mat tradition. For not only has Faqir detailed his spiritual quest with disarming frankness, but also he has also in uncompromising terms revealed the illusory nature behind many religious visions and miracles. Quite simply, his work is without parallel in the history of *nirguna bhakti mysticism.*

Professor Bhagat Ram Kamal of Government College (Hamir Pur, Himachal Pradesh) has done most of the translation work. My edited copy of the same was proofread and approved by Dr. K.L. Jaura, the Administrator (at that time--1980) of the Faqir Charitable Library Trust in Hoshiarpur, Punjab, India. I have kept my editing to a minimum so that the simple charm of Faqir's words would be kept intact. At times this makes for some unusual neologisms (such as Faqir's use of "gurudom") which may make a few sentences sound a bit awkward. Instead of "polishing" Faqir's rhetoric too much, I decided that I would sacrifice "correct" English for vernacular charm. I realize that several of Faqir's claims (such as a human simply being a transformation of a sperm--he leaves out the importance of the female's egg) are not scientifically accurate. But we must keep in mind that Faqir was not well educated--at least not in any formal way--and that his views have a deeper message, regardless of their factual content. I say this precisely because Faqir would be the first one to revise his views in light of the latest scientific discoveries. I think the intelligent reader can decipher the overall point that Faqir is making and not get bogged down with the limitations of Faqir's analogies or metaphors. Moreover, we must always remember that Faqir is stressing his own ignorance, and it is that very ignorance which is the essence of Faqir's preaching. Concerning the spelling of Indian terms, especially technical terminology used in the Radhasoami tradition, I have decided to use a rather haphazard method. For instance, Faqir would spell "Radhaswami" with a "w" instead of the more commonly accepted "o" ("Radhasoami "), "Hazur" with an "a" instead of a "u" ("Huzur"), and "Swamiji" with a "w' instead of an "o" ("Soamiji"). Since there has been a heated controversy over the spelling of Radhasoami terms in certain branches of the movement (especially in Soami Bagh), I have simply let both spellings remain whenever they occur. At first this may confuse the reader, but I think that there are some important historical reasons not to alter Faqir's original spelling. This also holds true for the capitalization of certain terms, such as God, Guru, Shabd, etc., which is not always uniform. Since Faqir himself approved the English translation of his Urdu autobiography, I felt that it would be better to retain his method of capitalization, even though it is not consistent Keeping these small discrepancies in mind, I don't think the interested reader will have too much trouble understanding the gist of Faqir's message.

Rarely, if ever, have we had a guru of Faqir's stature admit so openly the evolution of his spiritual understanding, especially when that very understanding ends not with claims of perfected knowledge but unqualified unknowingness. As Faqir Chand said several years before his death,

"Who knows what may happen to me at the time of death? I may enter the state of unconsciousness, enter the state of dreams and see railway trains. . . How can I make a claim about my attainment of the Ultimate? The truth is that I know nothing."

With such a profoundly open outlook, one can only wonder if the unknowing sage melted into the empty luminosity or into the dream world of running trains."

Foreword by Dr. K.L. Jaura

The autobiography before you is a clear account of Baba Faqir Chand's life. In general, self-narratives paint only the bright side of the picture, ignoring the darker aspects of life. But Faqir presents both parts and offers a complete view of his spiritual struggles. This is the unique quality of his life story which separates it from others of its kind. Indeed, Faqir has laid down only what he has practiced himself. In his autobiography almost every incident is followed by the effects it had on his life, the lesson drawn from it, and in turn how it became part of his teachings. It has added a desirable depth to the book.

On behalf of the Faqir Library Charitable Trust, I deem it necessary to add here, in brief, an account of Faqir's research and teachings in the spiritual field, besides the activities started and maintained in the *Be Man Temple* under his divine guidance. Whereas on the one hand, on the basis of his life long research in the quest for enlightenment, Faqir throws a new penetrating light on the subject of Self Realization and the final goal Nirvana, on the other hand, he has brought revolutionary alterations in the prevalent principles and teachings for humanity in general. The education he imparts to the common man derives from the need and the spirit of the present times.

Every saint comes to this world with an exceptionally kind and sensitive heart. How could Baba Faqir Chand remain unaffected by the "devil dance?" (The massacre which occurred during India's partition in 1947.) Deeply perturbed he observed a fast for two days and engaged himself in deep meditation. He came out after this with a key message of "Be Man" to humanity. And in order to place before mankind his advanced realization for the benefit of the world, Faqir founded *Manavta Mandir* (lit, "House of Man") at Hoshiarpur in 1962. This was the first center of its name and kind in India.

According to Faqir, to be a true man one must have or earn the supreme jewel of discrimination. The wisdom to know the false from the true, the shadow from the substance, the fleeting from the permanent, and the reflection from the primordial cause. His daily satsangs in Manavta Mandir went a long way to help seekers in this regard. In fact, such is the quality of Faqir's analysis that an average reader is able to see and grasp clearly apparent complex riddles of human existence.

Enlightened souls take birth in this world at crucial times in history in response to the pleas of suffering humanity. These Divine physicians come, observe the situation, and then diagnose ways whereby the ailing masses can recapture the lost paradise of mutual love, happiness, and peace. Such ones come not to divide but to unite. They practice, preach and establish universal brotherhood. Their work knows no boundaries, whether geographical, political, or of caste, creed, or color. But when they *Die to Live* in their immortal abode, their closest disciples under the intense feelings of gratefulness and attachment for the physical form of their late masters, lay foundations for new sects, religions, and creeds. This they do mainly to perpetuate the name and fame of their spiritual guides. With the march of time these religions and sects fall into the hands of worldly men, who being ignorant begin to behave as if the Guru and the sect were ancestral property. As a result, the selfless and enlightened service to humanity is replaced by exploitations of the ignorant in the name of religion. Man fights man. Mother earth gets divided into different countries and provinces.

Just consider, what greater injustice is possible to those perfectly realized emissaries of God than to confine their teachings to sects, cults, and religions and fan the flames of hatred, prejudice and bias amongst the human race. The ideal welfare for all humanity is ignored while Satan dances triumphantly in the name of God.

Baba Faqir Chand, true to the lineage of Satgurus, has reached the conclusion that the cause of all in fighting and suffering amongst religious peoples is ignorance of the real concept of Master (or Guru) and based on it the misconceived Master/disciple relationship. According to Faqir, the real guru is the knowledge, the sense of discrimination, and the understanding given to the seeker by a realized One and *not* the man who imparts this truth. The human frame of the outer guru is mortal, whereas the real Master never dies. Faqir appeals time and again to the religious leaders all over the world (in his numerous published talks and conference meetings) to understand the wrong turn the Guru/disciple relationship has taken. By mistaking the Master to be human, the real guru--the knowledge imparted--is lost.

Remembrance

ॐ

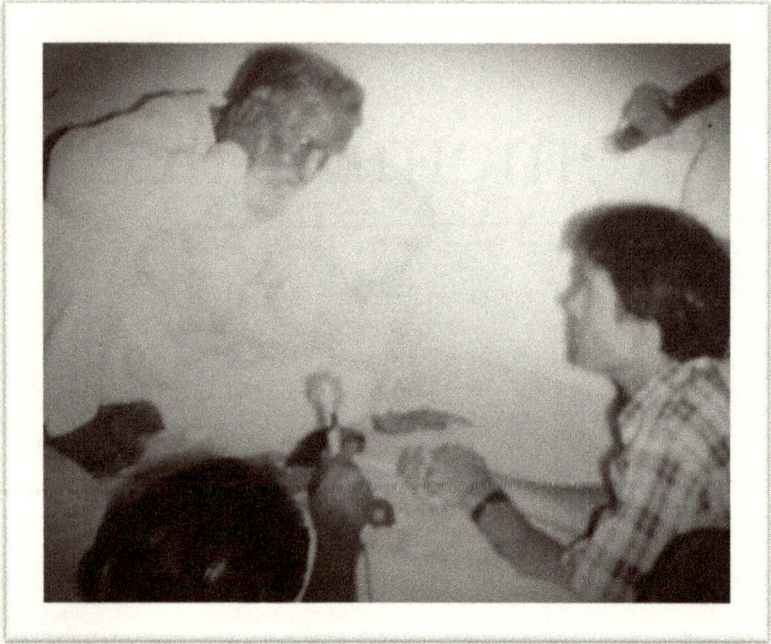

याद

A Personal Recollection

I first learned of Baba Faqir Chand in the Fall of 1977 when I was looking through the card catalogs at the U.C.L.A. research library for my genealogical work on the Radhasoami tradition. I found an obscure book by Seth Achal Singh entitled *World Religious Conference, Delhi/ 1957*, listed under the unclassified section. After tracing the book, I noticed it contained two striking pictures: the first was of Pratap Singh, the then current Satguru of the Namdhari Sikhs; and the second one was of Faqir Chand. I immediately surmised that this Faqir must be the same one mentioned in Agam Prasad Mathur's *Radhasoami Faith: A Historical Study* that I had read earlier. [1]

I subsequently wrote to the sage, wondering if he was still alive. The only address I had was "Manavta Mandir, Hoshiarpur, North India." To my joyful surprise, in less than four weeks I received a letter from Faqir Chand along with three books, including one entitled *Light On The Anand Yog*, written by his, guru, Shiv Brat Lal Varman. [2] Seven months of continuous correspondence followed. Finally I asked Faqir if I could visit him when I came to India in the summer of 1978 as a Research Assistant to Professor Mark Juergensmeyer (University of California, Berkeley) who had received a grant to study the Radhasoami tradition. My job included visiting the various gaddi nasheens (spiritual heads) in the different sangats. Faqir kindly agreed to my request, cabling me to come direct from Delhi when I arrived in India. [3]

I still vividly remember my first trip to Hoshiarpur. I stood in the crowded Delhi train station trying to figure out how I could secure passage on the train when an Indian gentleman behind me asked me about my travel plans. I hesitated, thinking that he would know nothing about Faqir or the "Be Man Temple." I was wrong. When I mentioned the saint and my destination, his face lit up and he said excitedly, "My grandmother is a great devotee of Faqir's; in fact, the guru will attend my sister's wedding in a few days. I will cancel my earlier train ride so I can go with you and guide your way." [4]

Although I never did meet the mysterious gentleman again, he did help me arrange my passage and told me something of the interesting city of Hoshiarpur which is near the foothills of the Himalayas.

After an eight-hour train ride through the night to Hoshiarpur I took a bicycle rickshaw from the train station to Manavta Mandir. The scent of the morning air and the lingering dawn light through the clouds had a strange impact on me. I felt as if I had entered a forgotten homeland. An odd sense of deja vu affected me. I spotted a photograph of Faqir Chand inside the entranceway that immediately caught my eye. "Why does he look so familiar to me?" I pondered to myself. Then, at the moment of my arrival, an old devotee of Faqir's enthusiastically greeted me, saying, "We have been expecting you. You have come on a most auspicious occasion--Guru Pumima Day." I was immediately surrounded by a number of Indians who were quite eager for me to have the darshan of Faqir who was then in deep samadhi. [5]

At first glance Faqir Chand did indeed seem completely unconscious of this world. But when I bowed in front of him, he rose up fully awake and hit me on the back strongly with his hand, giving me an affectionate welcome.

Faqir's *Be Man temple* was unique. Instead of just pictures of gurus who belong to Faqir's direct lineage, there were photographs of masters from almost all of the Radhasoami lineages, including a huge color portrait of Sawan Singh, the late gaddi nasheen at Beas. Adorning the end of the hall was a life-size statue of Faqir Chand's guru, Maharishi Shiv Brat Lal.

After a little rest, I was invited to attend Faqir's morning satsang that was held outside due to the large crowd. The sevadars in charge kindly gave me a chair to sit on, since I was not used to sitting cross-legged. I can never forget Faqir's animated expressions during the satsang. As the crowd was singing shabds (hymns of devotion), Faqir with his eyes closed would swing his hands as if conducting a concert. Then after the completion of the shabds, Faqir spoke in Hindi about various aspects of Sant Mat. Surprisingly, given my limited knowledge of the language, I understood the gist of Faqir Chand's discourse--one which is echoed throughout his writings: "When I came to this line as a Guru my eyes were opened. Why? Because those who regard me as their Master my image appears to them in their meditation, in their dreams, and even in their state of wakefulness and guides them, whereas I remain unaware of all this. A lady sent me a letter stating that she was

2

having a bath in a river in Kashmir. Suddenly (she records) a wave of water came and took her away for ten or fifteen yards. She writes that when she was drowning I appeared there, caught her hand, and brought her out of the river and said, 'You have yet to do a lot of work.' She has written to me so as to know what work she is to do. Now neither did I go there to save her, nor did I tell her that she has yet to do a lot of work. This is the secret."

Later that same afternoon I had a personal interview with Faqir Chand which lasted several hours. Although Faqir's native language was Hindi/Urdu, he spoke fluent English so there was no need for a translator. I asked Faqir a number of questions which related to guru succession (i.e., how many other disciples besides yourself served as gurus after Shiv Brat Lal's death?), but he kept turning the discussion to a more personal side, asking me about my own meditation practice, ethical life, and so forth. Faqir was eager to share the gist of his own quest so that my own spiritual journey may be smoother. I had the sense during our conversation that I could ask any question that I wanted. One impression that has always stayed with me about Faqir Chand was his remarkable unpretentiousness. Despite his Brahmin caste, Faqir appeared to treat each and every individual as his dear son or daughter. In my case, due to my young age (twenty-two years old at the time), Faqir called me a "son, rather a grandson." His obvious warm regard and affection endeared him to me almost immediately. Below are a few questions and answers from that first interview:

Question: *When did you start working as a Guru? In 1918, or after your Guruji died?*

Answer: No, not during his lifetime and this (was) out of sheer veneration for him, even (though) I had his orders to deliver discourses and initiate people. He was running an ashram of his own. I wanted to speak the stark Truth. Though Hazur Data Dayal Ji had given hints about the Reality in his writings, verbally he did not always speak out bluntly. In his last discourse before death he made it clear that he did not project himself in the vision seen by his disciples. This secret he revealed only in the last discourse because if such things are told all too abruptly people would not come.

3

Question: *Was Nandu Singh commissioned by Shiv Brat Lal to do this work of Satsang?*

Answer: Yes, he too was commissioned by Hazur Data Dayal Ji just as I was. Nandu Bhai Ji was the disciple of Hazur Data Dayal Ji like me. But I joined in 1905 and he in 1919. Bhai Nandu Singh had his field of work in the Andhra Pradesh. Once I went to Nandu Singh's house. He was holding Satsang in his house. I told him that he should not hold Satsang in his house. When he inquired about the cause, I said to him, "Your form appears to your disciples; are you in the know of it?" He said, "No." Then I told him that those people would bring offerings to him just because his Form appeared to them in their Abhyas. So the offerings that he would get he would give to his children. Then there would be trouble to his children. After that he did not hold meetings in his house.

Question: *Is there anyone else commissioned by your spiritual father to do this work?*

Answer: I do not know. So far I am the first man, rather the leading one. There are others also. Even my own disciples are doing this work at different places in the country. I, for one, do not initiate people. I simply explain the Truth. Those who believe in my words are benefited. [6]

Faqir and I soon became fast friends. Each day he would talk with me for two or three hours about his spiritual realizations. One morning, however, was quite special. The old sage was lying down on his back in *samadhi* with a white sheet over him. For all practical purposes, at least to those devotees sitting next to him, Faqir Chand was out of his body, enjoying the bliss of higher inner regions. I was sitting in a western style chair in quiet observation when, to my astonishment, Faqir descended from his contemplative state, pulled down the sheet covering him and looked me straight in the eyes and said, "I want to speak with you!" What followed was one of the most penetrating and enlightening discourses I have ever heard, for, unlike most gurus in India, Faqir Chand revealed in detail the secret behind many inner visions and miracles:

"Now, you see no Jesus Christ comes from without in anybody's visions. No Rama, no Krishna, no Buddha, and no Baba Faqir comes

4

from without to any body. The visions are only because of the impressions and suggestions that a disciple has already accepted in his mind. These impressions and suggestions appear before him like a dream. Nobody comes from without. This is the plain truth. Look here. There is a woman. She has got a son. That child loves that lady as his mother. The child will have nothing in his mind against that lady. He will adore her; he will love her and respect her. The brother of that lady comes; he has different thoughts for her in his mind. When her husband meets her, he carries different feelings in his mind about her, and when a friend of that lady meets, his mind is different. From the same lady different individuals get different types of love, affection and adoration. So, whatever you have to gain, it is all with this faith and belief that your Ideal is perfect. Whatever you gain, you gain it as per your own faith and belief. As a child gets motherly love from his mother, similarly the husband gets a wife's love from the same lady. You always have this faith and firm belief that your Guru is within you. Do not think him ever away from you in any human form. Guru is Knowledge or correct understanding."

It was during my numerous conversations with Faqir that I learned of his radical understanding of the truth of our existence. Although Faqir taught the practice of *surat shabd yoga*, he also emphasized the importance of discrimination *Jnana yoga*). In personal letter to me, dated March 8, 1978, Faqir described the process for enlightenment:

"Whatever I have realized is that one should research his own self. Unless this done one cannot get peace. Nobody is in a position to know the secrecy of nature. I try to make a man realize Himself. Know thyself by thyself. To realize one's own self one has to penetrate within himself, leaving the physical, mental and spiritual senses. And what will remain behind is thy own self. And that self is eternal. Visitor of body, mind, and spirit, that self is a part of the infinity (which) no one can know except (he) lose(s) (his) own entity and merge(s) himself in the reality which is named by different sects and religions by different names. Some call it Allah; some call it Nameless, Formless, Akal, Anami, Ram or Radhaswami. Try to penetrate within yourself. Leave physical senses by repeating Holy Name given to you by your guru without moving your tongue. Meditate on the image of your guru. Concentration on the image is necessary for leaving mental vibrations. Then comes light and sound. Try to know what is that who sees light within or listens (to) sound within. Then one can realize who is he. His search ends and one becomes the same reality."

During my stay at Manavta Mandir, I had the opportunity to closely observe Faqir Chand and some of his personal habits. I noticed the following: 1) Faqir Chand did not live at Manavta Mandir, but made his residence in a small abode several blocks away from the ashram. 2) Faqir arrived very early in the morning at Manavta Mandir, usually in a bicycle rickshaw. 3) Faqir would go into *samadhi*, deep meditation, every day and his followers would sit around him also meditating. 4) Faqir Chand's withdrawal of consciousness was such that only the whites of his eyes would be visible. 5) Faqir smoked a huqqa, a water pipe filled with tobacco, in the afternoon, at which time he would also go through his correspondence. 6) Faqir was of small stature, though his health was exceptional for a man in his 90's. 7) At times Faqir's eyes would look as if they were deep ocean blue, and at other times hazel brown. 8) Faqir attracted a number of highly educated disciples, including university professors, lawyers, judges, and doctors. Devotees of other gurus respected Faqir's satsangs. I noticed that Faqir Chand had admirers from Beas, Agra, Delhi, Tarn Taran, and other Sant Mat centers-- several of whom I personally interviewed.

The last day of my stay with Baba Faqir Chand is deeply engraved upon my heart. Faqir was lying down in a back room when I was ushered in to pay my farewell respects. The old master took my face in his hands, looked intensely into my eyes and reiterated what he had said upon my arrival, "You are like my son, rather a grandson. I wish you to be practical in your life. There are two schools of thought. The aim of one school is to bring people into its circle. They bring people into their church. But I remove people from the church also. To be (born) in a church is a blessing, but to die in church is a curse. You cannot (fully) understand my views as yet, because you have to do a lot of work in your worldly life as yet. The present devotional ideas which you have now will change after some years, and then in your old age you will come to this line. This is my prophecy about you."

Faqir gave me a message to pass on to Maharaj Charan Singh of Radhasoami Beas, for whom he had the highest respect, since I was going to attend his satsang the following day. Faqir then went on to say things of such a personal nature that I keep them forever locked within myself. As I got up, after pronaming at his feet, I knew that I would never fail to remember the compassion and beauty of this great, "unknowing" sage of Hoshiarpur.

After my brief stay at Manavta Mandir in the summer of 1978 I never saw Baba Faqir Chand again. I had hoped to entertain the ninety-five year old saint in my home in September 1981 during his fifth United States tour. But two weeks before his planned visit to southern California, Faqir Chand suffered cardiac arrest, went into a coma and died three weeks later in a Pittsburgh hospital. I was blessed, though, with a telephone call from Faqir Chand a few weeks before his death but it was the last time I heard his radiant voice.

Faqir's death came as a shock to many of his Indian devotees. However, it appears that Faqir Chand knew of his forthcoming death. During a tape-recorded conversation a few days before his trip to America, the old saint was asked when he was coming back to India. Faqir, in an unusually cryptic reply, responded, "I will come back in a black box." And so it was. In the Fall of 1981, Faqir Chand's casket arrived at the Manavta Mandir ashram in Hoshiarpur, North India, for final cremation rites.

Since my visit to Manavta Mandir and reading Baba Faqir Chand's books many times, I became convinced that his life and work should be more known in the West. I was pulled to share his realizations primarily because they shed a clearer, more sure light on the spiritual path. Devotees of each and every line of spiritual practice--from *surat shabd yoga* to *Advaita Vedanta*--I felt could benefit from the keen, perceptive, and, above all, frank insights of Faqir Chand. His wealth of experience in the realm of meditation, so honestly and painstakingly revealed, is of unique advantage for scholars interested in transpersonal psychology or consciousness studies.

As I write these last sentences I do so with the deep sadness that one of the greatest yogis of the 20th century is no longer physically with us. Perhaps the best tribute we can bestow on Faqir is to truly learn the message that he lived and preached for over fifty years:

"The malady, the ills, and the sadness human society suffers from are not because we do not remember God or do not go to the temple, or Mosque or Church or to a Gurdwara, but because man does not learn to Be-Man in the correct sense. . . Therefore, my advice to all those who seek entrance into Sant Mat and want to transcend the inner stages of spirituality is: first of all make sincere efforts to become a man in the real sense of the word, because a pure mind is the prerequisite for

spiritual advancement. This is why I have named my ashram Manavta Mandir in Hoshiarpur. We can only be spiritual if we are true human beings first."

NOTES

1. Namdharis are a subsect within Sikhism which believes in a living guru and follows a strict moral code, including abstention from meat, alcohol and tobacco. This "Pratap Singh," the late head of the Namdharis, should not be confused with Sri Pratap Singh, the deceased leader of the Radhasoami Satsang in Tam Taran.

2. Steve Morrow has since edited *Light On Anand Yog* for publication by the Sant Bani Press in New Hampshire (now under the title *Light On Ananda Yoga*).

3. During this period I received six letters from Baba Faqir Chand; two of them were over fourteen pages.

4. It may be just an unlikely coincidence but my trip to Hoshiarpur was filled with a number of unusual events. See the book, *You Are Probability* (MSAC Philosophy Group, 2014)

5. In the latter part of July, religious Indians celebrate "*Guru Purnima Day*" which is a special occasion for disciples around the country to express their respect and gratitude to India's gurus and masters.

6. *The Master Speaks To The Foreigners: Seekers From Abroad* (Hoshiarpir: Faqir Charitable Library Trust, 1978), page 18.

Introduction to Unknowingness

Note: *The following introductory essay was originally written in the 1980s and is an attempt to reconcile Faqir Chand's unknowingness hypothesis with claims made by a select few gurus who claim to have knowledge of some bilocations. My own views on the subject have evolved over the years and I find myself more and more convinced that Faqir's view is more universal in its import than I originally suspected.*

After meeting personally with Baba Faqir Chand, it became exceedingly apparent to myself and Professor Mark Juergensmeyer (who visited Manavta Mandir in late August of 1978) [See Juergensmeyer's book, *Radhasoami Reality* (Princeton University Press, 1991)] that the old sage was something of an anomaly amongst Indian gurus. For, although Faqir Chand had a rather large and devoted following (numbering in the thousands), he absolutely disclaimed himself of any miracles attributed to his spiritual work, saying quite frankly that they were products of either the devotee's previous karma or intense faith. Indeed, it was this very insight that led Faqir to his own enlightenment.

When Faqir Chand began to initiate disciples into *surat shabd yoga*, at the request of his master Shiv Brat Lal, a most curious thing happened. His devotees began reporting that Faqir's radiant form appeared inside their meditations. Others related miracles that were caused by Faqir's prashad (blessed food), letters, or advice. However, all during this time Faqir claims that he had absolutely no knowledge or awareness of his form appearing to distant provinces or performing miracles to the sick and dying. As Faqir himself wrote, "People say that my Form manifests to them and helps them in solving their worldly as well as mental problems, but I do not go anywhere, nor do I know about such miraculous instances." [Faqir Chand, *The Essence Of The Truth* (Hoshiarpur: Faqir Charitable Library Trust, n.d.1976?)] It was at this point when Faqir asked himself, "What about the visions that appear to me? Are they a creation of my own mind, and does my guru also not know about his appearances to me?" Only then, according to Faqir, did he realize the truth: "All manifestations, visions, and forms that are seen within are mental (illusory) creations."[Faqir Chand, *The Secret of Secrets* (Hoshiarpur: Faqir Charitable Library Trust, 1975)]

After his realization, Faqir began preaching his belief that all saints, from Buddha, Christ, to even his own master Shiv Brat Lal are ignorant about the miracles or inner experiences attributed to them. In a paper given to the *American Academy of Religion* in March 1981, I used the term "The Unknowing Hierophany" to describe what Faqir Chand believes; that is, a "Divine" vehicle within the temporal world that is unaware of its spiritual manifestations. [A revised form of this original paper was published under the title "The Hierarchical Structure of Religious Visions," in *The Journal Of Transpersonal Psychology* (Volume 15, Number 1)] Though Faqir is probably the most outspoken, other great religious leaders, saints and mystics have expounded on this same unknowingness. However, it is not seen by most (especially devotees) as an explanation of their subservience to the Great Mystery, but rather as a statement designed to exhibit the saint's humility, or as a tacit attempt for concealing his real mission and purpose. Jesus, for instance, is reported in the *Gospel of Mark* as asking the crowd that was following him, "Who touched me?" After this, a woman who had suffered from a flow of blood for twelve years came up to Jesus and told him about her plan for a Divine cure. By a brief touch a miracle happened, as she was cured from hemorrhaging. At this Jesus said, "Daughter, your faith has made you well." [*Saint Mark*, translated and edited by D.E. Nineham (Harmondsworth: Penguin, 1976)] The famed sage, Ramana Maharshi, when asked about Jesus' power to perform miracles, substantiates what Faqir Chand had taught for over forty years: "Was Jesus aware at the time that he was curing men of their diseases? He could not have been conscious of his powers. Such manifestations are as real as your own reality. In other words, when you identify yourself with the body as in *jagrat*, you see gross objects; when in subtle body or in mental plane as in *svapna*, you see objects equally subtle; in absence of identification as in *sushputi*, you see nothing. The objects seen bear relation to the state of the seer. The same applies to visions of God." [*Talks With Sri Ramana Maharshi*, Volume I, II, and III. (Tiruvannamalai: Sri Ramanasramam, 1972), pages 17 and 355]

Along with this "unknowingness" there is also the internal, ever-present supreme knowledge that saints and sages have described as the hallmark of enlightenment. Jesus said, "The

12

Father and I are one." The Sufi martyr, Mansur al-Hallaj, shouted before his execution, "ana'l-Haqq" (I am the Truth). Sarmad, the Jewish-Indian saint, exclaimed, "I am King of Kings." And Meister Eckhart, in slightly different language wrote, "The eye with which God sees me is the same eye which I perceive Him." These quotations illustrate that mysticism is concerned with spiritual knowledge: the relationship of the soul with God, and not with any secondary psychic abilities which may arise as a result of intense spiritual discipline. However, this kind of knowledge cannot be equated with logical, objective learning. The former is the realization of one's eternal nature, a transcendental experience of oneness. The latter is concerned with dualistic thinking, knowing about things--that which is based upon an illusory division of the world into two separate components: the subject and the object. Thus, when saints talk about the ultimate knowledge, they are referring to the Ground of Being, that which is the condition for all subsequent conditions. Consequently, an enlightened master may not know anything about academic subjects such as quantum mechanics, anthropology, or critical history. As Ken Wilber astutely comments, "I have yet to see a guru run a four-minute mile with his `perfect body' or explain Einstein's special theory of relativity with his `perfect mind'. . . Perfection lies only in conscious transcendence, not in concrete manifestation." [*Spiritual Choices* (New York: Paragon House Publishers, 1987), page 258]

Even though Faqir Chand was not conscious of his miraculous powers or his healing gifts (nor, evidently, are most other gurus), does it necessarily hold that all masters are likewise ignorant about their visionary manifestations? Moreover, is it true that all religious visions are individual creations, determined by the faith and concentration of zealous devotees? At first glance, the answer would appear to be "yes," because many internal visions are not of factual and historical human entities, but of amalgamated characters, mythic beings, and fictional heroines--some whose life stories may be entirely based upon the writer's own creative mind.

For example, Paul Twitchell made up the literary figure, Rebazar Tarzs, claiming that the Tibetan monk was over 500 hundred years old and resided in a remote region in the Himalayan mountains. Although Rebazar Tarzs does not, in fact, exist, devoted followers of Paul Twitchell's religious movement, Eckankar, claim to have extraordinary visions of him. What is transpiring is fairly obvious: when one ascends to a different level of awareness (like in O.B.E.'s or N.D.E.'s) they interpret the inner light according to their own particular cultural background. Sikhs see Guru Nanak, not Moses; Catholics see the Virgin Mary, not Buddha; and Eckists see Rebazar Tarzs, not the store clerk at 7/11. [For more on this phenomenon, see my chapter, "Gakko Came From Venus: The Invention Of A Religious Tradition," in *Exposing Cults* (new edition, forthcoming). However, on closer inspection it becomes apparent that some masters claim to know about their subtle interactions with disciples and that certain visions may not be merely due to extreme faith or concentration. This psychic awareness, as it were though, apparently arises spontaneously and is not the product of any sustained conscious manipulation.

A classic example of a fully conscious bilocation experience comes surprisingly enough from Ramana Maharshi, a sage who did not show even the slightest interest in psychic powers or abilities. Recounts Arthur Osborne, Ramana's biographer:

"About a year after his meeting with Sri Bhagavan, Ganapati Sastri experienced a remarkable outflow of his Grace. While he was sitting in meditation in the temple of Ganapati at Tiruvothiyur he felt distracted and longed intensely for the presence and guidance of Sri Bhagavan. At that moment Sri Bhagavan entered the temple. Ganapati Sastri prostrated himself before him and, as he was about to rise, he felt Sri Bhagavan's hand upon his head and a terrifically vital force coursing through his body from the touch; so that he also received Grace by touch from the Master." Speaking about this incident in later years, Sri Bhagavan said, "One day, some years ago, I was lying down and awake when I distinctly felt my body rise higher and higher. I could see the physical objects below growing smaller and smaller until they disappeared and all around me was a limitless expanse of dazzling light. After some time I felt the body slowly descend and the physical objects below began to appear. I was so fully aware of this incident that I finally concluded that it must be by such means that Siddhas (Sages with powers) travel over vast distances in a short time and appear and disappear in such a mysterious manner. While the body thus descended to the ground it occurred to me that I was at Tiruvothiyur though I had never seen the place before. I found myself on a highroad and walked along it. At some distance from the roadside was a temple of Ganapati and I entered it." This incident is very characteristic of Sri Bhagavan. It is characteristic that the distress or devotion of one of his people should call forth an involuntary response and intervention in a form that can only be called miraculous. [Arthur Osborne, *Ramana*

Maharshi And The Path of Self-Knowledge (Bombay: Jaico Publishing House, 1982), pages 93-94.]

Ramana's experience of bilocation indicates that Faqir Chand's categorical statement about all gurus not knowing about their visionary manifestations may need qualifications. Simply put, some saints appear to know about their miraculous appearances. The number of these "fully aware" mystics, however, is so incredibly small that it is not an exaggeration to say that Faqir Chand's "unknowing" hypothesis explains almost all of the so-called guru visions in the world. The overwhelming majority of inner visions are projections of one's own mind which have no substantial "reality check" with either the outer world or the higher inner regions. Furthermore, the object of devotion in these transpersonal encounters are, for the most part, not aware of their role. Thus, the *Chandian Effect* is a general explanation that covers almost all transpersonal visions. Ramana's experience and others like his represents a very small, bracketed, "special" case scenario. As such, it warrants further inspection, but should not be misconstrued as a general reference point with which to adjudicate transmundane happenings. The *Chandian Effect*, so named because Faqir Chand was the first Sant Mat guru to speak at length about the "unknowing" aspects of visionary manifestations, designates two major factors in transpersonal encounters: 1) the overwhelming experience of certainty (*ganz andere/mysterium tremendum*) which accompanies religious ecstasies; and 2) the subjective projection of sacred forms/figures/scenes by a meditator/devotee without the conscious knowledge of the object/person who is beheld as the center of the experience. [I first coined the term in my article, "The Himalayan Connection: U.F.O.'s and The Chandian Effect," *The Journal Of Humanistic Psychology* (Fall 1984).]

Concerning these "special cases," Sawan Singh, a deeply admired master in the surat shabd yoga tradition (1858-1948), for whom both Faqir Chand and his teacher Shiv Brat Lal had tremendous regard, wrote that the outward guru can and does know about the inner condition of his disciples. This knowledge, Sawan Singh pointed out, is conveyed to the physical master via the inner Shabd (Divine Sound), though only in extreme cases where the outer master's attention is needed. [See Sawan Singh's letters to American and European disciples in *Spiritual Gems* and *The Dawn of Light* published by the Radhasoami Beas Satsang.] Writes Sawan Singh to one of his disciples:

"Now regarding your question about the Inner Master and that Inner Master guiding the disciple, first of all, what is the Inner Master? The Real Saint or Perfect Master is one with the Supreme Lord, having merged His Being with the Supreme. Now, as the Supreme Lord has all power, so do the Perfect Masters. He can do as He pleases, and anywhere and always, so that He may better work with, protect, and instruct and guide His disciples. Every time He gives the initiation to anyone, He creates an Astral Image of Himself in the disciple. And from then on, the Master never leaves the disciple. The Double, or Other Self, or Image of the Master is sometimes what we call the Inner Master. Now, if anything occurs in the life of the disciple that requires the personal attention of the Master, here (in India) in the Body--this Inner Master at once reports to the Conscious Master (in India) and the Conscious Master gives the thing his personal attention. The Master sometimes calls these Doubles of Himself his agents. They do his work, taking care of all his disciples. They have the power to act without limit. They can do what the Master wishes Them to do, and They obey His orders. The human side of the Master here (in India) may not know what is going on in the life of that person. It may be on the other side of the globe. He will not be aware of the details, but He can know them if He wishes. But manifest-ly, you see how difficult it would be for any one man, as man, to go to all parts of the world and take care of so many. If the Master had a million disciples, He would have an Astral Double of Himself in every one of them, and that Agent of the Master would look after the disciple at all times, reporting to the Master here (in India) only in case of extreme emergency." [Extract From A Letter By The Great Master To A Disciple, *Science Of The Soul* (June 1985)]

Hence, according to this perspective, the outward master does not know most of the time. Similar to Ramana Maharshi's experience, the Beas master learns of his visionary manifestations on only special occasions. The modus operandi behind how certain masters could possibly know about their disciple's spiritual experiences is explained in a remarkable passage by Da Kalki (alias Da Love Ananda; Da Free John; Bubba Free John; Franklin Jones): "After that time, [when Da Free John achieved Enlightenment] when I would sit for meditation in any formal way, instead of contemplating what was arising in myself, I would contemplate other beings as my own forms. Instead of my own psychic forms arising, the psychic forms, minds, and limitations of others would arise. I was aware, visually and otherwise, of great numbers of people, and I would work with them very directly on a subtle level. In some cases, these people would soon contact me and become involved with me in a personal relationship. Others were people I already

16

knew. I would work for them in the subtle way, and then watch for signs and demonstrations in their outward lives of the reality of that manifestation. I tested everything in this manner." [Bubba (Da) Free John, *The Enlightenment Of The Whole Body* (Clearlake: Dawn Horse Press, 1978), page 38.]

My citation of Da Kalki should not be construed as an endorsement of his mastership; it is not. Although I am sincerely a great "fan" of Da Love Ananda's writings, I am a very harsh critic of his personal lifestyle. I have written an extensive article on this very point--how to distinguish the message from the medium--because it is vitally important to remember that a superb writer/thinker does not mean that by extension that the person is "God-Realized" or a "Perfect Master." Moreover, I am not all that sure that Da Kalki has any psychic experiences. I just happen to think that his explanation of possible psychic experiences is clear and rational. [See "The Paradox Of Da Free John: Distinguishing The Message From The Medium." *UCSM* (Volume One, Number Two).]

Charan Singh, the late head of the Radhasoami Satsang at Beas, for instance, chose disciples for initiation by simply looking at them. I have personally seen thousands of people file directly in front of Charan Singh and in a matter of a few seconds he turns his head to the left or to the right, indicating whether the seeker was accepted or rejected for Nam-Dan. [Nam-Dan is a ceremony where the living Satguru gives the "Gift of Nam" or Initiation to chosen disciples. It includes precise details about how to meditate and withdraw one's consciousness from the physical body by means of a three-fold method: simran (repetition of holy name(s)), dhyan (contemplation of the inner light or the guru's form within); and bhajan (listening to the divine sound current). There are several movies that have filmed this unusual selection process for Nam-Dan, including Satguru (London 1976), *The Dera Documentary* (Dera Baba Jaimal Singh, Beas, India, 1970's), and *Guiding Light* (Dera Baba Jaimal Singh, Beas, India 1983). I personally witnessed the event inside the famous Satsang Ghar at Dera in the Winter of 1981.] Needless to say, it is an awe-inspiring sight, and one which I confess is beyond my limited comprehension.] During his second world tour in 1970, Maharaj Charan Singh was asked the following question: "Is the physical Master aware of all the initiates' inner experiences?" Charan Singh's answer demonstrates that the outer master does know about his visionary manifestations.

Responded Charan Singh: "Our real Master, as I just told you, is the Shabd and Nam. And when we are connected with that Shabd and Nam, that Shabd and Nam takes care of us. The physical Master, of course, is aware of all that. [My emphasis.] But, you see, it is Shabd and Nam which is our real Master, that takes care of everything." [*Thus Saith The Master* (Beas: R.S. Foundation, 1974), page 150.]

Another example of extraordinary manifestations which go beyond Faqir Chand's hypothesis of unknowingness comes from Baba Jaimal Singh, the first guru of the Beas satsang and a personal disciple of the founder of Radhasoami, Shiv Dayal Singh. In the following excerpts, Jaimal Singh details a most remarkable physical bilocation of his guru. Recollects Baba Ji:

"Once, during Christmas, the army units were allowed four holidays. As I had no official duty assigned to me during that period, I felt that I could best spend it in meditation in my room. Accordingly, I told the cook that I should not be disturbed, that if I needed food I would personally ask for it. Also, if anybody asked for me, he should be told that I was out. It so happened that soon thereafter my presence was required for writing some accounts. However, as my door was locked, everybody who came to call me went back disappointed. Meanwhile, the officer of the Unit had demanded full account from the clerk who really did not know what to do in my absence. Just when a thought crossed his mind that he should report my absence to the officer, he saw me and heard me say to him that he should take down the account. This the clerk did. Such accounts were rendered three times daily, and were thereafter sent to the officer concerned by the clerk immediately after he got them. This continued on all the four days during which I was engaged in meditation in my room. However, I knew nothing about it, for I would leave my room only at four o'clock in the morning and ten o'clock at night just to answer nature's call. When the holidays were over and I came out of my room, I was called in for accounts for the day previous only. I explained to the clerk that I had been confined to my room for the last four days and had not given any accounts at all for the entire period. The clerk then called the two persons who had been present at the time the accounts were rendered. One of them even produced the paper from which I had actually dictated, saying that I could myself ascertain whether this was the account written by me in my own hand. When I examined this paper, I found it to be exactly what it should have been. I silently meditated upon Huzur Swami Ji's Feet and bowed in gratitude for His unbounded Grace in representing me during my absence and carrying out the job assigned to me for that period." [Baba Jaimal Singh, *Spiritual*

Letters (Beas: R.S. Foundation, 1984), pages 13-14. In the same book Jaimal Singh relates several other extraordinary bilocation experiences.]

Although Jaimal Singh's experience was extraordinary, there have been other reports by mystics of similar physical bilocation excursions. [See D. Scott Rogo's *Miracles: A Parascientific* Inquiry *Into Wondrous Phenomena* (New York: The Dial Press, 1982), Chapter IV, which deals specifically with bilocation experiences around the world.] The important point to remember, though, is that such experiences are the exception, not the rule in mysticism. The value of Faqir Chand's revelations of ignorance is that most gurus (I am tempted to say all) in India and elsewhere are in the same lot, but falsely parade their attainments to sincere, if gullible, disciples. Faqir's startling insights show that most religious visions are, in fact, products of one's own mind. When I use the term "mind" here it should be equated with "imagination." Naturally, all visions are of the mind in the strict sense of the term, but those manifestations which cannot be correlated by others either in this world or the higher worlds are, for the most part, merely vivid extensions of one's imagination.

However, we should not take Faqir's confessions as precluding the possibility that certain rare saints do have access to knowledge far beyond our comprehension, and that being residents of those higher regions have the ability to directly transmit such information to their respective followers. [If I may interject a personal note here, I must confess that I find myself more and more agreeing with Faqir Chand and his claims of unknowingness.] As a seasoned observer of the guru scene, most of what I discover is petty human motivations. To be sure, there are gurus who have deeply impressed me with their compassion and humility (Charan Singh being, at least for me, the most impressive), but I have yet to unearth an airtight, empirical case for genuine psychic powers. There are always some uninspected loopholes that reveal that natural (versus supernatural) processes were involved. I realize that my skepticism will turn off a number of parapsychology buffs, but in light of Occam's Razor I see no overwhelming evidence to suggest that Faqir Chand's autobiographical admissions are not right on the mark.

Moreover, we should keep in mind that Faqir Chand's use of the term "ignorance" has two meanings. First, Faqir uses the term in an absolute sense equating "Ignorance" (with a capital "I") with God, thereby agreeing with many saints and mystics that the Lord is an unqualified Mystery (as Shiv Dayal Singh put it:

"Wonder, Wonder, Wonder; Wonder hath assumed a form"). In this reference, there will most likely be little debate with Faqir Chand. However, Faqir also uses the term "ignorance" to describe his realization that gurus do not know about their visionary manifestations. As we have noted, there may be exceptions to this general rule, though they have yet to be empirically verified

The Life

ॐ

जीवनवृत्त

The Life

1

I was born on November 18, 1886, in a Brahmin family in the Hoshiarpur district of the Punjab. My late father, Pandit Mast Ram, was an employee of the Indian Railway Police. He being the only earning member of the family and his pay being very small, financial poverty ruled our household. Moreover, maybe due to the nature of his work and/or his monetary worries, my father's disposition was very strict. Tormented by the poverty at home and always fearful of my father's wrath, from the age of seven years onward I sought relief in the name of God. My thoughts and actions were virtuous and in the course of time I studied the *Ramayana*, the *Mahabharta*, and other scriptures of Hindu Dharma. From these works I developed a love for the incarnations of Rama and Krishna and meditated upon their forms.

2

I studied up to the middle standard at Pind Dadan Dhan in the Jhelum district (now in Pakistan) where my father was posted. However, due to lack of resources my education could not go beyond the middle class. At the age of eighteen I got employment as a signaler in the Construction Line of the Indian Railways. During off duty hours I learned telegraphy privately with the help of a signaler at the railway station. At this tender age I came in contact with the Contractors of the department. They were all meat eaters and their company turned me also into a non-vegetarian. Due to my association with these people I took to other wrong ways as well. I ate meat for six months; drank rum on three occasions; gam-bled once and lost one rupee and a quarter, and also once visited a prostitute.

3

It was an extremely cold morning in 1905. The previous night a terrible earthquake had shaken the whole Kangra district causing a tremendous loss of life and property. My cousin, true to his daily routine, got up in the early morning hours, took his bath in ice-cold water, and said his prayers. After his devotional, he prepared the meals and we sat down to eat it. At this very time, an employee of the railway station came in and placed a plate of meat before me. My cousin, who was a vegetarian, felt repelled by the foul smell of the dish. He put both of his hands on his mouth and nose, and, out of hatred for the meat, threw two chapattis on my plate. He was shivering. I could not ignore the dramatic reaction of my relative. This gave rise to a discussion within me. I thought: "He is my cousin. He is following the dictates of Hinduism and leading a pure life, whereas my actions are in the opposite direction. Why is this so?" For half an hour a mental conflict continued within me: should I eat the meat or throw it away? [Meat eating is a highly undesirable act for a Brahmin.] Ultimately I decided not to eat the meat and abstained from non-vegetarian foods for six months thereafter. All this time I was full of repentance over my falls from the dictates of Hindu Dharma. Soon after my act with the prostitute I realized my weakness for sex and wrote to my father requesting him to send my mother and my wife (I was married at thirteen) to live with me.

4

One day I was going for a walk. On the way I happened to meet a Jangli village headman. In the course of our conversation we started to discuss the pros and cons of meat eating. He put his arguments in favor of meat eating so logically that I forgot about my previous repentance. Before leaving the headman handed me a chicken. A class IV employee beheaded the little creature and prepared it for cooking. I asked my wife to cook it. When my mother learned of this, she went inside the kitchen and bolted the door from inside. My wife knocked at the door of the kitchen, so that she may cook the meal. But my mother would not open it. Then my elder brother and I pounded at the door requesting her to open it. Frightened because there was smoke coming out of the kitchen, I broke open the door with an axe. My mother came out. The suffocating smoke in the kitchen, anger, and disappointment over my accepting the meat loomed large over my mother's face. Overpowered by affection, I embraced her and implored, "Why did you not open the door? Had you been suffocated to death, where could I have found you dear mother?" My mother, out of sheer anger, pushed me away and fell down to the ground. I rose up, and under the prevailing affection of my heart, again embraced my mother and asked her why she was so angry with me. Then she said, "You have killed the baby of a mother. The mother hen must be wailing over the loss of her dear child. You have committed a terrible sin." At once, prompted by my conscience, I made a firm vow that in the future I would never commit such a sin.

5

For earning pardon for the four sins I had committed I prayed to God in the form of Rama and Krishna. I prayed and wept very hard. I was helpless to do so. I wanted my mental slate clean and it was not possible until my transgressions were eradicated. Perhaps my tears, shed so profusely, spoke of my conscientious desire to be purified.

My peace of mind was disturbed. I felt restless most of the time. It was a moonlit night. I was praying to the Lord and weeping bitterly. There appeared before me an aged sadhu with a long gray beard and a tambura (guitar) in his hand. Most lovingly he asked me, "Dear child, what makes you weep? 'I have committed four serious sins. I have known from the Hindu scriptures that God takes birth in the human form in this world. I want to see Rama and get myself pardoned for my sins,'" I said. The kind, old sadhu assured me thus, "For you, your God in the human form is already on this earth. You will come into His contact and all your sins will be pardoned." After saying these words the sadhu disappeared. Following this incident, my impatience to see God face to face increased.

6

In the meantime I got a permanent job in the Indian railways and was posted as Assistant Station Master at Baganwala. But my craving to see the Lord did not diminish; rather, during this time it reached its peak. Once I wept for twenty-four hours continuously for a glimpse of the Lord. Doctors were called in. They administered medicine to me. At about five o'clock in the morning I saw in a vision the form of Maharishi Shiv Brat Lal. He drew water from a nearby well and helped me take a bath, and then told me his address in Lahore. I also saw my father in the appearance and he made com-plaints before Maharishi Shiv

25

Brat Lal against me. Then a class IV employee woke me and this vision came to an abrupt end.

7

This experience convinced me that God had incarnated Himself in the form of Maharishi Shiv Brat Lal. So I started to write one letter every week and send it to the address that appeared in my vision. Inside the letters I always addressed Maharishi Ji as God. For ten months I regularly wrote to Shiv Brat Lal. After this period of nearly a year, I received a letter from Maharishi wherein he wrote, "Faqir, your letters I have been receiving regularly. I value your sentiments and your passion for the Lord. 1, myself, have discovered Reality, Truth, and Peace at the feet of Rai Saligram Ji of Radhaswami Mat. Provided you feel no reluctance in following this path come and see me at La-hore." My craving to see God in the human form had reached its fulfillment. I had previously submit-ted an application for leave some time back. As per His Will, the same day that I received a letter from Maharishi Shiv Brat Lal a station master reached Baganwala and told me that he had come to relieve me. What a coincidence it was! I handed over the charge to him and left for Lahore the same day.

8

I reached the ashram of Hazur Data Dayal A (Maharishi Shiv Brat Lal) and prostrated my humble self at His Holy Feet. He gave me an exceptionally affectionate welcome and initiated me into Radhaswami Mat. His Holiness gave me a book and asked me to go through it. The work was *Sar Bachan* written by Swamiji Maharaj (Shiv Dayal Singh), the founder of Radhaswarni. I went through some pages of the book in the very presence of Hazur Data Dayal Ji. But I could not pursue it any further, though, because Swamiji Maharaj had most vehemently criticized almost every religion, including Vedanta, Sufism, Islam, Jainism, and Buddhism. He declared them all to be Kal and Maya. It was too much for me. I felt hurt and tears rolled down my eyes. His Holiness noticed my reaction and inquired for the reason. I broke out, "Hazur, God is One. I have faded to understand the justification for condemning all other religions as incomplete. This is a direct attack on the religion of my ancestors." Hazur very lovingly advised me, "Keep aside this book and never read it until I ask you to read." Maharishi instead gave me two other books, one on the life history of his guru, Rai Saligram. Maharaj Ji, and the other by Kabir Sahib entitled *Kabir Sakhi*. He advised me to attend the satsangs (meetings) of Radhaswami Mat wherever available.

The spiritual practice, as directed by Hazur Shiv Brat Lal, became part and parcel of my life. As I was not yet adept in the inward practice of ascending the higher stages of light and sound, I remained satisfied with my concentration on the Holy Form of His Holiness Data Dayal Ji.

9

On my way back from Lahore I used to stay at Malkway Railway Station. There a book stall agent used to give discourses on Radhaswami Mat. Once the agent refused to share his huqqa (an Indian smoking pipe used for tobacco) with me. "We are both Brahmin by caste, why have you refused to share your huqqa with me?" I inquired. He surprised me by responding, "Babu Kamta Prasad Sinha (alias Sarkar Saheb) is the only true incarnation of Radhaswami Dayal." [Babu Kainta Prasad Sinha was at that time head of the Radhasoami Satsang at Ghazi-pur in Uttar Pradesh.] He meant thereby that I had not been ini- tiated by a true guru and thus was not a true satsangi. I very politely said to him, "Dear brother, God is one. He belongs to all and all belong to Him. He may manifest to his devotees in different forms at different places and different times. But if you do not agree with me, then let me write a letter. You mail this letter to your guru. His reply in any form shall be accepted as final and I shall abide by it." There and then I wrote the letter, shedding tears of love and devotion for the Supreme Lord and handed it over to the gentleman to post it to his guru. After fifteen days I was told that Babu Kamta Prasad Sinha had breathed his last and should wait for a reply until his successor was chosen. From this incident I concluded that followers of Radhaswarni Mat [Ghazipur] were not impartial and true seekers of the ultimate reality. Their approach towards the all-embracing Truth was narrow and very sectarian. Hence, I gave up their company and avoided all blind followers thereafter. Even if anybody wished me "Radhaswami," I responded with "Ram Ram."

10

In 1916, during the First World War, I volun-teered myself for war services in the field in order to earn more money and repel the pressure of poverty from our family. Before leaving for my post on the war front I went to Hazur Shiv Brat Lal for His Blessings. He gave me the book *Sar Bachan* (which he showed me on my first visit to him) and advised me, "Study this book now and devote more time to *simran* (repetition of a Holy Name or Names) and *bhajan* (listening to the inner Shabd, the Audible Life Stream)." Thereafter I left for Baghdad where I was to be posted. During my stay in Baghdad I threw myself wholeheartedly in spiritual sadhana. I gave as much time as possible to inward practice (meditation) and led a life of complete celibacy. These sincere efforts of mine with a desire to know the Truth bore fruit and in the course of time I ascended all the inner regions and experienced the lights and sounds at each stage on the inward path. These inner fruits of my meditation filled me with joy and ecstasy. But in spite of this achievement I was not yet con-tented, because I wanted to realize the Truth which had prompted Swamiji Maharaj to condemn all religions.

11

Towards the end of 1918 1 was granted annual leave and I went home to India. I went to His Holiness at Lahore to spend my maximum time in His company. During my stay with Hazur Shiv Brat Lal I always troubled him with never ending questions and queries. One day I placed before Hazur the main agony of my heart in these words, "My Lord, I have traversed many inner regions of Sant Mat. I have dwelt in the Light within and have experienced Shabd (the Sound Current) in indescribable abundance. No doubt, these experiences have been a great source of joy for me. But, still I long to see myself and know the sublime goal of Radhaswami Mat. How and why does the goal of Radhaswami Mat differ from that of other religions? I yearn to experience the supremacy of the Radhaswami faith myself." His Holiness assured me that he would answer my question the next day.

My anxiety increased and I was very eagerly awaiting the next day. It was December 25, 1918. Hazur Data Dayal Ji called me in his room. I was already waiting for the moment. I went inside. Lo! His Holiness with a strange blend of affection placed in my hands one coconut, five [coins], made a frontal mark on my forehead and bowed himself to my feet saying, "Faqir, you are yourself the Supreme Master of your time. Start delivering spiritual discourses to the seekers and initiate them into the path of Sant Mat. In due course of time, your own satsangis will prove to be your 'True Guru,' and it is through your experiences with them that the desired secret of Sant Mat will be revealed to you." Touched by these words, I experienced both joy and sorrow within me. Hazur noted both expressions on my face and asked for clarification. I humbly said, "Your Holiness, I am myself ignorant of the Truth, how can I lead others on this sublime path? And when the thought that I have become a degree holder and would deliver discourses and initiate people flashed within my mind, I felt that I had become something and thus a spark of joy." Hazur then said, "Faqir, you may be suffering from ninety-nine shortcomings, but one sure virtue of Truth which is within you will lead you to your goal in life. You will not only redeem yourself but will help many others to attain release." I spent my entire leave at the Holy Feet of Data Dayal Ji and then left for Baghdad to join my regiment.

12

In Baghdad I used to sing devotional songs. Every fiber of my being became saturated with a passionate longing for the Ultimate Truth. I always felt over-flowing with love for my Lord, Hazur Shiv Brat Lal, who was for me an incarnation of Rama. My devotion transformed my personality and made me a center of attraction for other spiritual seekers in Baghdad. I came to be regarded as a mahatma, while some chose me to be their spiritual master.

13

In 1919 1 was posted in Iraq. The aboriginal inhabitants (known as Baddus) revolted, which led to a fierce battle, I was inspector in the department of telegraphy in the railways with my headquarters at Divinia. The rebels made a heavy attack on the Hamidia railway station, killing the entire staff and setting the building on fire. Military forces from my post were rushed to Hamidia. I was also ordered to take charge of the Hamidia railway stations as Station Master. Our soldiers laid down wires in trenches and occupied their positions. Fierce fighting continued and there was a heavy loss of life on both sides. At Hamidia we were left with a group of thirty-five soldiers and one Subedar Major. The rest of the army was sent to Divinia to retaliate any attack there. With the fall of the night the rebels attacked us. Our soldiers, though less in number, fought back. One of our men was wounded while casualties on the opposition were very heavy. As the firing ceased for some time, the Subedar Major came to me and asked that I convey to our headquarters at Divinia that we were short of ammunition. And, if we had to face another such attack, our supplies would not last for more than an hour. If the ammunition supply failed to reach us before dawn, none of us would be alive. I wired the message to the headquarters accord- ingly. The situation was tense and everybody was feeling as if the end had come. I too was shaken with the fear of death. In this very moment of fear the Holy Form of Hazur Data Dayal Ji appeared before me and said, "Faqir, worry not, the enemy has not come to attack but to take away their dead. Let them do that. Don't waste your ammunition." I sent for the Subedar Major and told him about the appearance of my Guru and his directions concerning the enemy. The Subedar Major followed the directions of my Guru. The rebel Jawans came and carried away their dead without attacking our positions. By six o'clock in the morning our airplanes came and they dropped the necessary supplies. Our fears vanished. We gained courage. We were safe.

14

After about three months the fighting came to an end and the Jawans retired to their barracks. I returned to Baghdad, where there were many satsangis. When they learned of my arrival, they all came together to see me. They made me sit on a raised platform, offered flowers, and worshipped me. It was all very unexpected and a surprising scene for me. I asked them, "Our Guru Maharaj is at Lahore. I am not your Guru. Why do you worship me?" They replied in unison, "On the battle field we were in danger. Death lurked over our heads. You appeared before us in those moments of danger and gave us direction for our safety. We followed your instructions and thus were saved." I was wonder struck by this surprising explanation of theirs. I had no knowledge of their trouble. I, myself, being in danger during those days of combat, had not even remembered them.

This incident caused me to question within myself, "Who appeared to them? Was it Faqir Chand?" My faith was strengthened and I concluded, "Whosoever remembers God in whatever form, in that very form He helped His devotee." This gave a new turn to my conception of the Spiritual Master. Henceforth I came to believe that the Master is no separate entity. Rather, He is the disciple's Real Self and resides within. Happy with this conclusion I came to India on annual leave in 1921.

15

With all my love and devotion I reached Radhaswami Dham. in order to worship my spiritual guru in person. I meekly presented at his feet one singhasan (throne), a set of bro-caded clothes, and a huqqa made of silver--all of which cost thousand of rupees. I worshipped His Holiness in a mood of supreme gratitude and ecstasy. I stayed with Shiv Brat Lal Ji for about forty-five days. During this time Hazur wrote down for me many poems in order to dispel my ignorance. At that time I did not understand them. Thou be a Faqir, be a Faqir, be Faqir my brother! I may swim across with they feet; 0! Faqir Blissful! I am not a devotee of Rama, Krishna; know not Brahm nor God! I have a madness for Faqir's name; I accept it alone as Supreme!

Hazur wrote the preceding simply to lift me up from my passive thoughts, because I used to consider myself as the greatest sinner. In another poem he assigned me dime duties: Thou has come in human form; wearing the garb of a Faqir, Take with thee miserable men; and lead them to the Guru's abode Man, weak, helpless and ignorant, is grieved by the continu-ing torture, by duty is to be compassionate; impart to people the True Name, 0 thou generous one. Since his command it has become my mission in life to perform these three duties: 1. Your name is Faqir, Be True to your name. Do not look at the faults of others. Instead have pity upon the helpless, ignorant and the weak. With your love and affection help them out of this sphere of Kal and Maya, guiding them to their real Home. 2. You have come blessed with a form which is really unique and wonderful. Your mission is "welfare of the humanity." Remove the walls which divide mankind and tell the whole world how it can live a happy and peaceful life. 3. Liberate the deserving amongst them from the cycle of life and death. Be their guide and take them to the supreme state of Nirvana.

16

In 1922 1 went back to Baghdad. For about seventeen years (up until 1939) 1 stayed away from delivering spiritual discourses. However, if any deserving individuals approached me for guidance, I did initiate him, and told him to concentrate on the Holy Form of Hazur Data Dayal. I stopped giving satsangs. Why? I thought that if I were to deliver spiritual discourses I must say the Truth, at least up to the point that I knew it. If I were to remain true to my conscience and rise up to the expecta-tions of Shiv Brat Lal Ji, I had to reveal the secret about the manifestation of the Guru's form to his devotees in moments of physical, mental and spiritual difficulties. And if I did that, the love, devotion and faith (blind faith) of people for His Holiness would be reduced. The offerings in cash, free and voluntary service, and the like by the disciples of Radhaswami Dharn ashram may also come down to a painfully low level. Thus I willfully waited for the proper time to come, so that Maharishi Shiv Brat Lal's ashram may not suffer any loss due to me. Ever since 1919 1 had a very strong desire to disclose the secret and let the world know about all types of manifestations within and without.

17

In 1938 before His Holiness shed off his mortal frame, I sent him a telegram with the following resolution: I solemnly promise that I shall spread the Truth to the world to the best of my ability and circumstances." Hazur left for his Sublime Abode in 1939.

Since his death I devoted all my possible time to simran, bhajan and dhyan. Thereafter I wrote two books, both commentaries. One on "Hidayat Narna," a chapter in *Sar Bachan Radhasowni Poetry*, written by Swarniji Maharaj, and a second on "Baramassa." Shortly after the publication of these two books, I presented two copies of each to Baba Sawan Singh Ji Maharaj of Beas. [Sawan Singh was the spiritual head of the Radhasoami Satsang Beas in the Punjab and was a close friend of Maharishi

Shiv Brat Lal.] Baba Sawan Singh Ji wrote to me, I have gone through the books. You are a true Faqir. You are doing highly desirable service to the Radhaswami Mat." But still I remained undecided about what I should do. Because I had a lurking fear in my mind that if I disclosed the Truth in plain words the narrow minded, orthodox, and illiterate amongst the satsangis would turn against me. Thus in 1942 1 got leave and went straight to Hazur Baba Sawan Singh Ji at Beas to explain my fears and difficulties in person. I had great reverence for Baba Sawan Singh Ji and I identified him with my Guru Hazur Shiv Brat Lal Ji. With utmost reverence I submitted to Baba A, "Your Holiness, kindly relieve me from the duty assigned to me by my Guru Maharaj. Pray, take this burden off my conscience, so that I may get released from the sin of disobedience of my Guru." His Holiness Baba Sawan Singh Ji placed his loving hand on my back and said ...... You do your assigned duty fearlessly. I shall be at your back under all circumstances." Since then I have been doing the work of satsang and writing books on my personal experiences and observations.

18

By 1942 1 had initiated about twenty-two disciples into the path of Sant Mat. Thereafter, I have not initiated anyone along the traditional method of initiation. Why? A lady form Jabbal accompanied by her husband and three children came to see me at Firozpur, where I had taken a service as U.D.C. in defense after my retirement from the Indian Railways. She was a great devotee and her spiritual practice was on the second center of meditation (i.e., Trikuti, the causal region in the terminology of the Saints), where she used to visualize my form in red light. As a result of this, she used to remain in a state of ecstasy. She said to me, "I want to devote more and more time to abhyas (spiritual practice) but my children take up most of my time and I feel disturbed." Her husband was a telegraph inspector. He would leave home at nine o'clock in the morning and return only at eight o'clock that night. Thus it was quite impossible for him to share her domestic responsibilities. The will power of the lady had immensely increased due to her regular concentration at Trikuti. As such, her desire to get more time for her spiritual practice had to be fulfilled. This is the law of nature. So, there was no way out except one: that she should be relieved of her children by nature. Before leaving me she bowed to me and I said, "Your wish will be fulfilled." When she left with her husband and children, I told my friend Pandit Wali Rain, who was sitting with me, that all the three children of this lady would die. My observations came true. Within a period of nine months all of the children died. I was shocked and thus I stopped initiation, except to those who had a pure mind and a strong desire for Self Purification.

Once I happened to visit Agra and I got one book entitled Prem Bani by the late Hazur Rai Saligram Maharaj. In the book it is written, "Persons with hatred, prejudice and selfishness in their minds can earn nothing but more sufferings, for themselves as well as for others by doing inward practice. But, one, with shortcomings and faults, who cherishes a strong desire to get rid of his shortcomings and faults also, would surely be benefited by simran, dhyan, and bhajan. The reason for this is that by daily practice of simran and regular concentra-tion, the win power of a devotee becomes strong and he becomes capable of overcoming his faults and weaknesses." Therefore my advice to all who seek entrance into Sant Mat and want to transcend the inner stages of spirituality is, First of all, make sincere efforts to become a man in the real sense of the word, because a pure mind is the pre-requisite of spiritual advancement. This is why I have named my ashram (center) Manavta Mandir (lit., "House of Man") in Hoshiarpur. We can only be spiritual if we are true humans first.

19

After my twelve-year stay in Baghdad I returned to India and went directly to His Holiness for Darshan. During my stay in Baghdad I had traversed many stages of Sant Mat and thus I was extremely happy and enjoying peace within and without. When I appeared before my Guru, he ordered me thus: "Faqir, since you have no male child, go home and beget one." I obeyed and reached my family. During my stay at home, I continued my abhyas and also enjoyed marital relations with my wife. I forgot the spirit of the advice of His Holiness and instead of going to my wife with the sole aim of begetting a child, I started to enjoy sex for the sake of enjoyment. This excess of indulgence in sex shattered my long earned joy and peace of mind. My digestion was upset and I suffered heavily both physically and mentally.

As a result I gave up taking grains, potatoes and rice for a long span of thirty-five years in order to regain my strength.

20

Once Hazur Data Dayal Ji sent two gentlemen to me. They wanted to understand spirituality. What is spirituality if not a happy life and a peaceful mind? At that time, I, myself, being bereft of that wealth, expressed my helplessness to them and asked them to go away. They wrote to Hazur about their visit to me and about my reply to them. His Holiness wrote back to them, "He who draws a blank from Faqir can only hope for nothing from me." After receiving this letter from Hazur Data Dayal they again came to see me. I read the letter and my mind revolted against guruism. But there was no way out. Tears rolled down my face and I lost myself in prayers. In mo-ments I lost consciousness of the world. During this time of absorption, I heard a voice from within me say "Lust and Peace never stay together." I got the answer to my problem as well as theirs.
Thereafter I controlled myself for the next twenty-eight years. I remained in the company of my wife, but sex had no place in our relations with each other. And in the course of time I regained my lost joy and peace.

21

In the human body semen is God in gross and visible form; Mind is God in subtle form; and Surat is God in causal form Those who do not know the art of moderate and controlled living all these stages can never attain peace. The seekers of spirituality must control their passion and protect their semen. [Here semen means the vital fluid--sexual energy--which is precious both to women and men.] Many young men and women come me for blessings. Why? They have not known the importance o celibacy. They waste their vital energy before attaining the age of maturity and thus they suffer from mental and physical ailments... To all young men and women, my advice is that they should lead their lives in celibacy. One should use his vital fluid only for begetting children and not for sexual pleasures. This is the lesson that I have derived from my lifelong experience and it has become the cornerstone of my life.

22

I have lived a very hard and honest life. My pay used to be very meager in those days and it was with great difficulty that I met my family's requirements. However, I did not adopt any unfair means to supplement my income. During off duty hours I used to work in a brick kiln near Miani Railway Stations. Shri Rain Ji Mal was the owner. He used to pay me five annas per one thousand bricks from the kiln. Then at the railway station, during my off duty hours, I used to work as a coolie. For carrying one item from outside the platform I used to charge one anna. I never had a feeling of inferiority in doing those odd jobs; rather my hard and honest earnings gave me inner strength and moral courage.

23

Throughout my life I have never used any undesirable method to supplement my income. Not to talk of accepting bribes (while there were many chances) in any form. I never used the official stationary for my private use. My father was Constable in the Indian Railway and ever since I came to age I stopped taking food at his place. Once, when my father was posted at Pind Dadan Khan Railway station, he fell ill. I came to him after crossing the river Jhelum. My father asked me to have dinner with him. I made an excuse and said that I did not have an appetite. After spending some time with my father I left and reached the Bazaar. There I had my meals at a hotel. In the meantime an old class fellow of mine came in the hotel and saw me eating there. He went to my father and casually told him that he saw me taking my meals in the hotel. My father felt very much annoyed and he came to me the next morning to know the mason of my eating at a hotel and not with him. I said, "Father, you are in the department of police and you accept bribes; therefore, I did not take food with you." From a worldly point of view this act of mine was not good. Perhaps I should not have done like this. It was nothing but my ego. But after this incident my father never accepted any bribe for the rest of his life.

24

I was married at the age of thirteen. in the hills the bride-groom is carried in a decorated palanquin. At the time of my marriage, I too was carried in a palanquin. When I was being carried I felt a great pleasure and prayed to God, "May I be married again, so that I may enjoy this pleasure of the palanquin again." The result of my prayer was that my wife died after sometime. My second marriage was arranged. I was again made to sit in the palanquin. Then the old scene of my first marriage flashed in my mind. I repented and, instead of enjoying the palanquin, I felt unhappy and sad. As you think, so you become. Your earnest desire is sure to be fulfilled; it may be good or bad.

25

I often ask parents that they should not beat their children, because I know the result of beating the innocent young ones. I was studying in the fifth class; I had my younger brother named Wazir Chand. He was very small and I had to carry him when my mother was cooking or doing some household chores. Many a time I was beaten for him. Once I was carrying Wazir and playing with him. Suddenly my foot hit something and I fell along with my brother. Wazir started weeping. My mother heard him and came running. She gave me five to seven blows as if it was my fault. My mother again put Wazir Chand in my hands and directed me to keep him in a playful mood. I came outside with my brother in my arms. I still remember the place where I stood and prayed to God in these words, "0! God, I am beaten for this child, either kill me or take him away." Within three months my brother died. My teachings are based upon my practical life. I do not say anything which I have not experienced or realized myself.

26

I was posted at Sunam Railway Station. One day, while sitting on a chair, I went into a deep trance. After sometime, when I came down to physical consciousness and opened my eyes, I found one handcuffed dacoit accompanied by a policeman sitting by my side. He was fanning me. I asked him, "Who are you?" He replied, "Maharaj, I am a dacoit." I said to him, "You are not a dacoit; you are a devotee." In a state of ecstasy I told the police- man, "He is not a criminal; you please set him free." It was a very hot day in the summer. Barefooted and bareheaded I left for SR's office which was situated in the market. Shri Bhagwan Singh was superintendent of police. When he saw me in such a state, he came out of his office and inquired as to why I had come to his office on such a hot day and that too barefooted and bareheaded. I told him about the criminal and stressed that he was not a dacoit and so wanted that he should be set free. The superintendent advised that this gentleman should become an approver and should tell everything; then he could to be set free. The advice of the S.P. was accepted. The gentleman was released. He promised to live a noble and honest life. I invited him to my home and served him food. He did live a changed and happy life.

27

In her old age my wife developed heart problems and some trouble in her teeth. Sometimes blood used to come out of her teeth. So during moments of pain, she occasionally used to say very harsh words to me. But I never felt her words, because Hazur Data Dayal's samskaras had a great impact upon my mind. Due to my spiritual bent, for a long time I had been indifferent towards my wife. Once I came on annual leave and went to His Holiness for Darshan. He directed, "Bring your wife alongside, otherwise I shall not meet you." Obedience to Data Dayal has been my religion. I went home and returned along with my wife to His Holiness. His Holiness said, I ask who is she?" I replied, "Hazur, she is the daughter-in-law of Pandit Mast Rain Ji." His Holiness asked again. Then I said, "Hazur, she is the daughter of Shri Surjan Ram R." Data Dayal asked me for the third time [sic]. I said, "Hazur, I have not been able to understand." Then His Holiness most compassionately said to me, "She is my daughter, if you hurt her you win hurt me." This samskara of Hazur Data Dayal Ji guided me in my family life and I lived very respectfully and peacefully with my wife.

28

Once I was coming to India from Baghdad on my annual leave. At Makina Camp I was waiting for the ship for my homeward journey. As there was yet some time for the arrival of the ship, I thought I would have some puffs of "huqqa" (tobacco). So I went to the kitchen of some labourers to collect fire from their place. The workmen had left for their earnings after finishing their meals. A four anna coin was lying near the fireplace. I looked all around (to confirm that nobody was seeing me) and picked up the four anna coin, collected the necessary fire for my "huqqa" and returned to my bed. When I reached my place, I thought, "You receive 500 Rupees per month. Why have you picked up this coin so stealthily?" I repented 'upon my foolish act and gave away that coin to someone. It is very easy to preach and sermonize others, but most difficult to be practical in one's life.

29

I was in the prime of my youth when I went to Baghdad. I stayed in Basra-Baghdad for twelve years. But I never went out to see the cities because the ladies of those towns had great beauty. Thus I avoided any visits lest my mind may not drag me down. One day I was sitting all alone in my quarter. The door of my room had a bamboo grill. From within my room I saw that two beautiful women were heading toward my quarters. These women generally used to visit our camp for meeting their friends and have enjoyment with them. On seeing the ladies at a distance I shut my door and sat inside silently. But after moments I got up and peeped through the door to see the women. What a pity! Who can believe the workings of the mind and who can dare to live free from it? This mind is not to be believed. It can bring you down to the lowest ebb in moments after taking you to the highest glory.

30

Once I was posted at Miani Railway Station. A train from Bhera arrived in. A young, beautiful and well-dressed girl also got down from this train. As I was on the gate, she handed over to me her ticket. But as I saw her, my mind went its way. In order to control my mind I slapped my face in the very presence of the girl. However, the girl went away. I did not know who she was. But the girl knew my mother. She directly went to my mother and told her about this incident. When I came home my mother inquired as to why I slapped my face when the girl handed over to me her ticket. I said to my mother, "Mother, now I am of age, please do not ask me such (a) question." Saint Kabir has written: I presumed mind as dead; it became ghost after death. Becoming ghost, it follows me; Tis such an undutiful son."

31

When I married I had a desire that my children should not have lust, anger, greed, attachment and ego. I wrote to Hazur Data Dayal about my desire and prayed for his blessings. His Holiness replied, "Whatever you wish shall happen." I was blessed with a daughter. At that time Hazur was away to North America. I visited his hut at Lahore and brought home all his worn out clothes because I was very much emotionally attached to Data Dayal and His belongings. I handed over those clothes to my wife and asked her to wrap the newborn child in them. The same was done. The result is that my daughter is as I wished her. She remains happy in the worn out clothes, whereas there is no dearth of new clothes for her. She would stitch the old ones and continue to wear them. Her mother died, but she expressed no attachment with her. This is the result of my own samskaras and desires for my child. Your thoughts and samskaras are carried to the womb of your wife along with your semen. You are responsible for procreating obedient, noble, wise, loyal and healthy children as well as disobedient and irresponsible ones.

32

I tell you another instance of my life regarding procreation of better children. I had no male child. I cherished a thought to procreate an honest, obedient, intelligent and noble son. I did get a son, who due to such virtuous and noble thoughts for him has never given me a chance of complaint till this very day. He is most sincere, obedient, and intelligent. He holds one of the top posts in a big government concern and draws about 3,000 rupees per month. He has so much regard for me that he does not sit in my rickshaw. He does not allow my servants to work for him. These instances of my life are being written for you so that you may learn some lesson of living a good and happy life.

33

During my visits to Hazur Data Dayal I used to trouble him too much, because I considered myself as the greatest sinner. But his Holiness always tried to lift me up from my negative and weak thinking. He used to say, "Faqir, you shall be the greatest among Faqirs." He always encouraged me and the result is my present position. He wrote a lot for me, but hereunder I reproduce (selections from) His last writing to me: "Who is happy in this world? Happy is only one, Faqir. What is this world? Tis a dream, and a dream too, for a Faqir. He dwells in ecstasy every moment, morning and evening. Faqir neither worships nor is worshipped. His is free from this show. Happy appearance, joyful heart, ever pure in his soul. Who you see in this state, accept him as a True Faqir. He is sage of both worlds, and a seer [sic] of two worlds. Whatever I have realized, I lay down here for thee. Thou had spread thy bossom [sic] cloth that is being filled today. Merged am I in my Self-, [Thee] too should merge one day. Ye shall attain thy destination; tis disclosed just today. That is why, above all others, I am proud of thee. Thou will illuminate the Nama--tis the voice of my heart."

34

In 1933 1 was posted at Sunam Railway Station. His Holiness Data Dayal visited my place. On the request of a large number of people satsang was arranged. In that general satsang Data Dayal said to me: "Faqir, the time shall change. The traditional way of preaching shall not be acceptable to the public. Therefore you must change the mode of preaching before leaving your physical body." In my obedience to the command of my Satguru I am obliged to speak out my experience and my research to the world.

35

Now at this age of ninety-four years, I live a life of peace and happiness. While knowing, I lead my life as if I know not. The entire creation is a game of one Supreme Power. Whatever we see, feel or know is a mere play of that Supreme Power. Whatever happens, good or bad (or beyond these both), is within His Order.

By His will man can achieve the state of Nirvana; and under His will man must continue to remain in the cycle of transmigration. To His will I bow, to Him alone I surrender. This is the last stage of my lifelong research. His will is Supreme. Whatever happens happened for the Good.

This belief gives me peace. By virtue of this knowledge I remain detached and do not identify myself with the trinity of body, mind, or soul. I always keep myself busy (work is a must in life) with selfless service to mankind in various ways. Inwardly I remain conscious of my Self and resigned (Sharan) to the Supreme Lord, beyond the regions of the gross, subtle, and causal.

The Teachings

ॐ

आदत देना

THE ETERNAL MYSTERY

I am not a Guru, nor have I ever desired to become a Guru. I did not want to do this work. I am bound to carry on this work as per orders of (my guru) Hazur Data Dayal Ji. I make no personal gains from this work. I do not accept anything from the public for my personal use or for my family. This gentleman (Sri Ram Ji Dass) offered me 500 rupees and some silver utensils to me yesterday. I said that I would not accept them. But I am to maintain his faith and love also. What I have done is to accept the offerings and give them in the marriage of a girl who is being married shortly. In lieu of it, I have paid 250 rupees from my pocket to the Manavta Mandir. I have nothing to do with utensils. But, my child, one thing I would like to tell you. I do not proclaim that whatever I say is correct or final. Whatever I say is the conclusion of my experience of life. Nature is unfathomable. No one has known it. A small germ in a body cannot know the whole body. Similarly (a) human being is like a small germ in a vast Creation. How can he claim to have known the entire creation? Those who say that they have known are wrong. No one can describe or even know the entire creation. Up to a certain extent to which man's mind has access, one can say something. But nobody can tell about the entire universe. It is indescribable.

BE MAN

Every individual on this planet is obliged to consider himself either a Hindu, Muslim, Sikh, or Christian, etc. The differences among individuals are based on religions. In addition to this there are other innumerable groups and parties based on economic status, social customs, cultural ties and different ideologies. As a result of these there are many divisions in the society and country. This attachment or affiliation to a particular sect, party or ideology makes an individual narrow-minded and prejudiced towards others and thus keeps him away from the Truth.

At the time of birth every child is free from any such religious ritual, social traditions, etc., and it is difficult to say with certainty which religion or sect that child shall belong to. He can be molded to any group from the people who nurse him.

Before discussing the real religion of humanity it is necessary to study some important facts about life first. What is man? Of what is he the product? Scientifically speaking an individual is an outcome of sperm from the semen. Semen is the product of blood, and blood is nourished either by the mother's milk or foreign milk which is nothing but the product of food stuffs eaten by the mother or the cow. Thus man, considered purely from the physical point of view, is nothing but a changed form of the products of earth.

Did that food in the form of blood, milk, and foodstuffs ever nourish him as a Hindu, Sikh, Muslim, or Christian? No. He is born simply as a child of man. This is not the work of any religion or sect. We are all born equal human beings, products of the motherland. Then, why these prejudices and jealousies among brothers and sisters of the same planet? All this proves that the basic and primary religion of man is *manavta* or Be-Manism. All other religions of today are the later product of man's thinking and his intellect but none of them is greater than *Be-manism* [be human].

THE GURU

One

What would you gain from the company of the Guru? You will gain the Secret, the Truth. But unfortunately every individual does not deserve it. Only rare personalities aspire for it. If you start teaching sexology to a child of six or seven years, will he understand anything about it? No, he will not. If you teach the subject of atomic energy to a student of eighth class, he will not understand it. Similarly, this Secret can also not be understood by every individual. There are stages and classes in each aspect of life. Therefore, I do not denounce anybody or any class. Every saint or guru is right in his own place. But only that Guru is not doing the right thing who does not speak the truth for his selfish motives, fame and name. Swamiji Maharaj writes:

Guru revealed now the Secret of the Unknown; surat ascended leaving the state of doubt. Realized the Secret of Separation; deviations ended of all vicissitude. Clouds of mercy started showers; the net of transmigration vanished. Broken the net of inaccessible; attained the pleasure with each breath. Attained today the fruit of Self-restraint. Mind became the Moth of the white. lotus. Burnt the sense of modesty and shame; cut the snare of rules and religion.

I myself was in the dark. I too considered (the) physical body as the Guru's fonn. In order to redeem me and to remove my ignorance His Holiness gave this task (of gurudom). I still remember the day when Data Dayal visited Giddarwaha. There I had said to my Guru, "Now you shall abandon your body." His Holiness laughed and said, "Yes, Faqir, whatever you have sai is correct. All my deeds have been exhausted but yours are st there. Continue doing this work. You shall have the glimpse of

Radhaswami Dayal in the form of your satsangis and you shall attain the Sublime State." I refused to do this work (of gurudom). My Guru again said, "You have not reached you esnation. This work shall redeem you." Now your (satsangis) kindness has redeemed me. Only due to you (Faqir is pointing to his disciples) have I been able to understand the Secret.

Now you yourself decide as to who is the servant of the Guru? He who serves Baba Faqir? Do you think he is the real servant? No. Only he is the real servant of the Guru who has the faith that his Guru is always within him. This knowledge shall help you at the time of death and not Baba Faqir. It is my word that shall lead you out of ignorance and illusion, and not me who remains at Hoshiarpur.

Two

It is said that Guru imparts Knowledge and the Guru is Shabd. Therefore, unless the surat of an individual ascends up with meditation to the state of Shabel, he cannot attain the true knowledge. Intellectually you may know everything from my satsang, but you practically shall remain ignorant. So never abandon your (meditation) practice at any cost. Sit for meditation for as much time as possible both in the evening and the morning.

Once I went to Lahore. I had an unflinching faith in His Holiness. Igot up early in the morning and did not do meditation. I still remember that scene. His Holiness came and asked, "Faqir, have you not meditated today?" I replied, "No, Maharaj, when I am sitting at your feet where is the necessity of meditation?" His Holiness laughed and said, "Practice daily, you shall realize the worth of this practice in your old age." Now I realize that whatever my Guru said to me at that time is perfectly correct. So mind it. Never miss your daily practice. Sit for as much time as you can.

What My Guru (ultimately) realized I do not know. I speak (only) of whatIhave understood. My Knowledge (Jnana) is that whatever buds forth or manifests within is nothing but illusion. The suggestions and the impressions are not the Real- ity. Until this fact is known the weight of existence does not vanish. After knowing that all the inward thoughts, feelings and manifestations are not a fact but a fancy, I do not get tempted by them. This is what I understand about True Knowledge.

So Kuber Nath (a devoted disciple of Faqir's) you came. I have given you the Satsang. Be happy. Whatever is within my control and whatever I can do, I do. I do not perform miracles. You believe me as your Guru. Therein is your redemption. His Holiness Data Dayal had once said, "Faqir, you have ninety-nine vices, but one virtue: Truth (Honesty)." The Truth is, however, that thy own Self is the Real Guru. I have spoken the Truth to you. Now it is your sweet will to serve me or not to serve me. I have done my duty. I have not deceived anybody. I have not kept anybody in the dark. Radhaswami to all.

THE SELF

One

(My disciples) experiences compelled me to dispel all mental visions and manifestations. I see the blissful Light and listen to the eternal Sound far beyond the state of thoughtless- ness. I always try to find out and recognize that object who beholds the Light and listens to the Sound within. But I have not been able to recognize it so far. It does exist. You are different from Light You are different from Sound. Now the question is if I have attained the supreme, unseen, and unbound state within, then I must have some extraordinary powers, so that I may be able to do some good to somebody, to the nation or to my self at least. But I cannot do anything. This proves that I am a mere bubble of Consciousness. Under His Will, from His Vibrations, this "I" was formed. "I" am neither God, nor saint, nor master, nor servant. "I" am a bubble that exists at His Will· and shall merge in Him at His Will, but I still fail to remain at this stage. My intellect still tries to know and identify "I" and know its master. This very search led me to Hazur Data Dayal Ji and now I am obeying him. I have no desire for name, fame and Guru- ship. I wish to merge in Him forever.

Two

I do not initiate anybody. People regard me as their Guru according to their faith. Sant Tara Chand Ji told me that I helped him in reaping his (farm) crops in the scorching heat. But I know that I did not go to help him.

To those who come to me with an idea of transforming their lives, I say accept the Supreme Lord in any form. Develop this conviction that He is the Supreme Worship. None except Him Alone. He who knocks at many doors gets nothing and remains restless. I do not plead to you to become followers of Radhaswami faith. Adhere to your own ideal according to your faith and remain attached to it till you are liberated from your illusive thoughts. I stand liberated from all religions. For me "Truth always wins," means the Supreme is an Element and none has succeeded to know Him.

I am nothing, but still I am every thing. I have been a son, brother, husband and father but I do not ensnare myself in this world of attachments. This is the essence of all the religions. But none tries to understand it. What is to happen must happen. Why make hue and cry?

Three

Whosoever would undertake sadhana of the higher stages beyond mental regions, forms, colors, and creations, shall see Light within. Light exists and manifests in everybody but its colors depend upon the nature of the individual. Some aspirants see red light within, others see green light and still others see sun, moon, stars according to their nature.

I know that I do not go anywhere; I am not aware of my manifestations. But satsangis tell me surprising incidents of my manifested forms. This experience helped me to see the Supreme Light within and attune myself to the Eternal Sound. I see this White Light in small as well as in vast regions. This Light that is within is Soul. The object that sees the Light within is something different. Man is constituent of body (gross matter), thought (mind), and soul (light). I have seen light of varied color within me. Many doubts used to lurk about the variety of these lights within.I have seen the sun, moon and enormous stars within from time to time. What were they? It was soul in different forms at different stages. At lower stages of sadhana when the soul comes in contact with subtle nature it represents itself in different colors at different stages. For example, in the material cosmos, the suns rises as purple red in the morning, at noon time it appears white, but in the evening it looks changed due to the effect of dust particles. The reality is that the sun is the same, its color is always the same, but it appears in three different colors at three different stages due to the effects of time and space.

A man who aspires to see his soul must follow the maxim "Truth always conquerors." He should detach his "Self ' from all worldly longings, cravings, and ego. After developing dispassion for worldly life, if he undertakes sadhana, he would easily be able to see the Light (soul). The object that sees the Light within is not to be named as soul. In Sant Mat this object is named as surat. This object/surat is part of the Supreme Surat (Super Consciousness), the Supreme Lord.

Four

The object that dwells in light and sees the light within yearns for something else. I am constantly trying to find out, what is it which aspires for a Higher Goal? This stage of "Something" is known as Chautha Pad (Fourth Stage), the stage of surat. When surat becomes alone during the course of regular sadhana after total withdrawal from gross and subtle existence, there develops an inexplicable condition in your Being. Hazur Data Dayal Ji writes about that stage: "Neither past, present nor future. Lamp off: light is gone."

THE GIFT OF NAM

One

I have been searching this Mine of Nam's gems since long ago and now I am eighty-nine years old. What did I find? If Shabd is considered the Nam (lit, "Name"; in this context it means the Divine Word or Supreme Logos) which is unbreakable sound (Dhunyatmak Shabd) then I dare not say it. Why? Because even after listening to that unbreakable sound, when I come down to the physical level, I still see visions. Many a time I see good scenes and sometimes bad scenes in my dreams.

This night I had a dream in which I saw running trains. An accident occurred; I carried my luggage; my father (whom I was afraid of) met me ahead. Then I met my mother, my first wife was also sitting there. I inquired from my wife, "What about your wounded leg? Is your leg now okay? Are you not my wife?" Meanwhile I awoke and attuned my Self to the Shabd (inner Sound Current).

From such experiences I came to understand that the mind of a man who undertakes the practice of *surat shabd yoga* (union of the soul, through the Sound Current, with God) does not become impregnable to the old samskaras. Do the old samskaras not magnify themselves in one's dreams? They do. During the last years of his life, when his brother expired, Data Dayal Ji wrote one of his dreams in a book. In that dream Hazur had written that he inquired from his late brother, "Where do you live?" It proves that even the saints of the stature of Shiv Brat Lal, Param Sants, Mahatmas and those who attune themselves to the unbreakable sound are not free from the influence of the old *samskaras*. They do bud forth in the subconscious mind of the great saints as well. All these deeds, thoughts and feelings where selfish motives are involved shall positively have their reaction upon the individual concerned, either in the waking state or in sleep. Why do I say so? This is my experience. Ever since the establishment of Manavta Mandir I have never dreamed about it. I have never seen Kuber Nath, Durga Dass, Munshi Ram, Gopal Dass or any other satsangi in my dreams though I meet thousands of them here and in my tours. Why? Because my Self is neither attached to Mandir nor to anyone of you. I have no selfish motive to achieve from the Mandir or through any of the satsangis. I have got good wishes for all of you and love for you. (But) I do not involve my Self in this game. This mother (pointing to an old lady sitting in the Satsang) looks after me, serves me and adores me, but she has never appeared in my dreams. But why my father, mother, wife and railway trains appear time and again in my dreams? Because my Self was attached to them. My Self had developed love for them. My Self had owned them. The impressions of ownership entertained by me for many years do not stop magnifying even today after a lapse of many years. What is the solution then to remove these impressions and free yourself from the grief, peacelessness and whims? If you are not free from them you are not liberated. What is that Nam which liberates you?

51

Kabir writes that mind is the cause of bondage and mind is the cause of liberation. If mind is all in all, then what does Nam do? Nam is the Experience, the Realization and the Knowledge which I have gained from your company. It is that I do not manifest anywhere. Whatever manifests within me or within you is not the Reality. Manifestations are nothing but the impressions and suggestions that are ingrained upon our mind and we have accepted them as Reality. Until an individual is firmly convinced that these manifestations and visions are only the reflections of ingrained impressions, the individual cannot attain Self Realization.   This is the essence of my research of ninety years.

Kuber Nath, you have come. I have love and good wishes for you. He came (indicating another man in the satsang). You serve me and he too serves me. This morning I questioned myself, "Have you attained Self Realization?" People say that the unbreakable sound within is Nam and generally this view is accepted. It is not so. This unbreakable sound is in fact a means to the ultimate. It is a means for the search.

Why did I make a search for Nam? I became introverted in search of "Something." I visualized forms [and] worshipped Rama, Krishna, Bhagwan and searched for the formless (nirguna) from within. During this quest I used to enjoy the glimpses of different forms and different scenes. I used to talk to these forms as well. What was all this? It was all the search of the mind. It was a search to find and reach that (real) Abode. I heard the tinkling of bells, blowing of the conch, saw light and heard sound within. Whatever I visualized and heard within was all a search of the mind. After having this long quest within I could attain Nam, and that too because of the experiences of (my) satsangis. Nam is nothing but the Experience, the Realization.

Two

Those who attune the Self to the sound and consider the sound as the Ultimate do not have Enlightenment; in fact, they too remain without the attainment of Nam. Why? I narrate to you an incident. What happens in dreams? I go to my bed, attune myself to the sound and develop an attachment with the Light within. But how long do I remain in that state? Ultimately I fall asleep and enter the state of dreams. Sometimes I become conscious that I am seeing dreams, but sometimes I do not. In my dreams I generally see trains, listen to the sound and see the

Light. Occasionally my wife, father, mother and rarely my son appear in my dreams. I see nothing more than them in my dreams. So if after listening to the sound current the experience is not gained about the reality of these visions, forms, and light, etc., the individual remains without Nam. This is my experience. I may be wrong. It is due to this fact that I wish the modern saints and mahatmas would speak (about) their practical life to their followers. I wish they would tell about how they face the realities of life in the twenty-four hour day.

So what I have understood about Nam is that it is the true knowledge of the feelings, visions, and images that are seen within. This knowledge is that all the creations of the waking, dreaming and deep sleep modes of consciousness are nothing but *samskaras* (impressions which are in truth unreal) that are produced by the mind. What to speak about others, even I am not aware of my own Self (in dreams). Who knows what may happen to me at the time of death? I may enter the state of unconsciousness, enter the state of dreams and see railway trains. . . How can I make a claim about my attainment of the Ultimate? The truth is that I know nothing.

After listening to this hymn of Hazur Data Dayal Ji, an idea struck within my mind, "You, Faqir, advise and preach to others, have you yourself attained Nam?" For me Nam is knowledge. The real realization of Nam is that the inner stages of Sahans dal Kanwal, Trikuti, Daswan Dwar, and Mahasunna are all Kal and Maya. They do not have an existence of their own, but are illusions. Whatever is seen within is one's own thought and one's own mind. It is your own mind that manifests in the form of Baba Faqir; your own mind solves your problems, but you give credit to me.

Three

Vyas Naryan, the astrologer, is sitting here. When he was in Ujjain my fonn appeared to him and solved many of his worldly problems. He came here and narrated to me all his incidents. I never knew him before. Now the question arises: Who manifested to him and solved his dilemmas? This is all the game of the mind and nothing else.

So my entire struggle has ended with this conclusion: the creations of the mind are ephemeral. They are reflections of the impressions and suggestions that are imprinted upon our mind. When the illuminating soul ascends to a particular region these impressions and suggestions get magnified and become visible within, just as the film is magnified with the help of a particular lens and focuses light in a cinema house. In a movie hall you see the running horses, fights, and dancing women on the screen. You enjoy the scene as if they are real. Many people feel happy when there is some good scene and weep when there is some tragic scene, whereas actually there is nothing on the screen except the magnified photos of a film. Similarly the ignorant feel happy or aggrieved by the inner mental visions. So Nam is the attainment of Gyan (Jnana), Knowledge and Equanimity. This state can be attained only by having a constant search within.

JIVAN MUKTI: LIBERATION WHILE LIVING

One

O Dayal' s mother, whom you see within and whom you love within is your own creation, your own child. You, yourself, create the image of Shiv Brat Lal in your center of Trikuti, while other devotees create ideals such as Krishna, Rama, or other Gods at the same center and enjoy their vision. Man is basically ignorant about the reality. Mother Bhagyawati is not a lonely example. I too suffered many hardships due to this very ignorance. Hazur, in order to dispel the fog of Bhagyawati, addressed her as mother out of compassion; and for the removal of my ignorance he deputed me for this duty of guruship to serve satsangis, so that I may realize the Truth. When you create my image for the fulfillment of your worldly desires and get many works done from my form, I remain unaware about such happenings. I daily receive a heavy mail about such miraculous incidents from satsangis. Such cases have convinced me that the manifestation of the Guru's form within me was not from without. It was the creation of my own mind. I do not go any-where, but my form does manifest at many places at the same time. It proves that it is one's own creation, one's own faith, belief and devotion. An individual enjoys visions within according to his intentions and convictions.

Two

The Holy Form that manifests within you is not that of external guru or ideal. It is your own Self. But your intellect cannot understand this truth because you have developed the belief that the manifestation of Data Dayal or of any God and Goddess is the reality. You make this center of meditation and remain attached to its joys. The object that visualizes the Guru or Ideal within is beyond your intellectual understanding. There is Light and Sound within you; the object that sees the Light and listens to the Sound is your Self. Your Self is the base and source of Light and Sound. . . Your intellect cannot help you realize the Truth because your Self is not born from your intellect, but your intellect is born from you.

Three

When a man realizes that birth, death, happiness or grief are all His sport (Leela) he remains undisturbed. He remains at His Will and enjoys bliss. This is the state of *Jivan Mukti* (Liberation While Living). I feel that the indirect method adopted by our saints is no more required in this changing world, so I have made use of the rod of Truth. My mission is not to entrap people with hollow words. This is a hard fact: the plain truth does not help in establishing centers; it does not increase the number of followers. But how is anyone to understand it (Truth)? Only after this realization: that he is a bubble of consciousness. A bubble of consciousness would not claim himself to be a yogi, sadhu or gyani. Had I not realized this Truth I might have made claims of my greatness and got myself worshipped from you and exploited you.

What was my form in the beginning? I say "I" did not exist at all. My existence is an outcome of an evolutionary process. Before acquiring this physical body, my original form was unnamed, formless, unseen, unsaid, limitless and profound. I have reached that stage from where "I" descended. Have I developed wings by becoming unnamed and unseen? Can I miraculously do any good for the suffering humanity? No. Let those who can make claims of their greatness do some good for the mankind. Who can say authentically that God is unnamed (Anami) or unseen (Alakh)? Man is in search of Truth. When his attention (surat) reaches or merges in its own self, he feels himself to be unnamed (Anami). He loses his "Self ' into a state of limitlessness and there ends his struggle of research. Who can know what man is? So, 0 man, none has known anything about God. All these pronouncers of different religious philosophies have no right to say that they have become something. Where did the immortality of Paltu Sahib go when he was thrown in the boiling oil pan? My Guru Data Dayal could not do anything against His (God's) will and save his ashram, Radhaswami Dham. Swami Param Hansa Dev, whose prashad had a power for curing incurable diseases, himself died of cancer. Saint Tulsi Das, writer of *Rama Charit Manas*, suffered untold hardships during his last three years. Awake! 0 man and understand what I say.

None on this earth can avoid His Will and neutralize the reactions of his deeds. You have been befooled and mercilessly looted by these so-called mahatmas and saints. You have not been made to realize your Self.

Four

The question arises that being the dweller of that Supreme State can I bring some miraculous change for the good of humanity? Nay, everything is pre-planned and pre-destined. I am not one to interfere or bring any change. At least two hundred barren women, many among them had no menstruation, begot male children with my prashad (blessed food). But contrary to it my own daughter has been married for the last fourteen years is still issue-less, whom I intentionally have given prashad many a time. What does this prove? I am none to bless anybody. Had it been so my daughter must have been blessed with a child. I can do nothing more than wishing good for all. My egoism has vanished.

Five

I am nothing more than a bubble of consciousness. I have not been able to reach His Abode so far. He is the Supreme Power and His end is beyond my reach. It is possible that Swamiji, Data Dayal Ji, Mohammed and other saints have reached His Abode or have known Him, but I have not. The feelings of the existence of self-power have ended and even the thought of liberation and bondage has disappeared.

Now mine is quite an old age. I am sure to leave this mortal world sooner or later. But where shall I go? I have under- stood that if I could remember Him, the Unnamed, the Formlessness and the Profound I shall merge in Him losing my own entity.

But if I remained attached to the worldly cravings or this gurudom, then I cannot say what would be my end.

Now I proceed to the immortal abode, breaking chains of all-- body, mind and thought. Follow those who desire our path of hanging on the gallows.

To reach that immortal Abode one has to dispel all worldly longing, thoughts, desires and attachments. Now what is meant by hanging on the gallows in Sant Mat? When someone is punished to death by hanging a rope is put around his neck from the gallows. The wooden plank is removed from beneath his feet and he is suspended in the air with only rope around his neck that throttles him to death. The accused gets no support whatsoever to his body except the rope of the gallows. Likewise, in Sant Mat, His Abode is the gallows. Surat or Self is to be hanged to it with simran, dhyan and bhajan (spiritual sadhana, interior meditation) and later to be suspended without any support of desire, longing, or even that of simran, dhyan and bhajan, except with the string of love. This is what I understand from the word gallows.

O' Faqir these satsangis have taught you the method of hanging at the gallows. Only this experience of the manifestation of my fonn at different places, of which I am never aware, has changed my life. . . My experiences prove that Yogi, Meditator, Guru, Disciple and even the aspirant of salvation are in bondage. Bondage means attachment of our surat (attention) with something, be it gross, subtle, or causal. Devotees of God are attached to their devotion and lost in it. They too are in bondage; the only difference is that some attachments are a source of joy, whereas others prove to be a source of worry.

These people who create my fonn with their mental forces to fulfill their worldly desires are not interested to know the Truth. They do not hang themselves on the gallows because they depend on the support of my Form, whereas to a man on the gallows there is no support. This is the highest stage.

Six

Long ago I used to pester Hazur Data Dayal Ji. One day after feeling greatly disturbed, His Holiness asked me to accom- pany him to Agra so that he might offer me to the Memorial Samadh of His Guru, Rai Saligram (in Peepal Mandi). I agreed. We reached the railway station and purchased tickets for Agra. Again Data Dayal said, "I shall be free from you after offering you at the feet of Hazur Maharaj (Rai Saligram). 'Will you not bring me back?'" I humbly inquired from my guru. "No," responded His Holiness. Then I said, "I shall not go to Agra and will not leave you." We went to the hermitage after returning the tickets. Inthe ashram of my Guru Data Dayal my preceptor said to me, "Faqir, I went to the Durbar of Hazur Maharaj only three times in my life and understood the Truth. I do not know why you are not understanding?" I again humbly inquired, "How did Hazur Maharaj make you understand?" My Guru replied, "I had questioned Hazur Maharaj how this world was created." My Guru asked me to look attentively at him. I obeyed. His Holiness opened his mouth and closed it and said, "This is the creation." At the time of the narration of this incident by Data Dayal Ji I could not understand it But today I understand. "Lips open and closed Tis the secret of life." Now I understand that all the lower centers (or inner regions from Sahans dal Kanwal to Bhanwar Gupha) are not the Reality. It is all phantasmagorias.

How did my delusion perish? First, this realization that I do not manifest anywhere removed the darkness of my mind. Second, when I ascend to the state of Light and Sound I try to search out the object which sees the Light and listens to the Sound. But I fail to find its end. It is infinite. What did I understand? Have I attained some extraordinary powers by reaching that state? No. I cannot treat my own ailments. Neither I nor any other saint could and can do anything. I reached this conclusion that this is all His Will.

The Interview
ॐ

भेंटवार्ता

The Interview

Editor's Note: Professor Mark Juergensmeyer, who is Professor of Professor of Sociology at the University of Santa Barbara, interviewed Faqir Chand in August of 1978 at Manavta Mandir. Professor Bhagat Ram Kamal of Government College, Hamir Pur, Himachal Pradesh, transcribed the interview and published it under the title, *The Master Speaks to the Foreigners*. The following edited version contains corrections (and explanations) which were not present in the original published interview.

Mark Juergensmeyer: As I have come here, I would like to ask you something about your development in spiritual understanding. First, you were a disciple of Swami Shiv Brat Lal?

Faqir Chand: Yes, I am a disciple of Maharishi Shiv Brat Lal. You have seen His Statue there installed in the hall. He is my spiritual Father. His spiritual Father was Rai Sahib Salig Ram, who was a Post Master General. Rai Salig Ram Sahib was the disciple of Radhaswami Shiv Dayal Ji, but I have got liberal ideas. I was born in a Brahmin family. From the age of 7 years there was a craving in me for something Unknown which I used to call Rama, Krishna or God. Now I feel that the Unknown thing which I wanted or searched for was Peace, but, at that time, I used to worship Rama, Krishna, God or Goddesses.

Mark Juergensmeyer: Where was this place? What place was this?

Faqir Chand: It was at my village Bhanjal, then in District Hoshiarpur and Punjab State. I have been doing worship from my childhood according to the ideas given to me by my parents. When I was 16 years old I joined service. I passed only my middle school examination. My father was a constable in the Railway Police. He could not give me higher education. So I joined communication service. There I met permanent way inspectors and contractors of all types. I was alone in the Communication section. In the society of those inspectors and contractors I took to wrong ways. I ate meat for 6 months, drank rum three times, once even gambled and lost one rupee and a quarter and once I went to a prostitute. You understand what I am telling you? In 1905 when the Kangra Valley was ruined by an earthquake my thoughts changed. After going to the prostitute I wrote to my father that I had done such and such wrong things, so please send my wife. I was married when I was only 13 years old. At that time I was meditating on the image of Rama and Krishna, according to the Hindu philosophy. When I was at Baganwala Railway Station as Assistant Station Master Lord Krishna used to be with me, whether I was working or walking.

Mark Juergensmeyer: Did you ever go to some Krishna Temple?

Faqir Chand: No. I used to pray to him within my own mind. I never went to any place. Once I was going and Lord Krishna was going ahead of me. There was some cow dung lying on the ground. That image of Lord Krishna asked me to eat that cow dung. I took a morsel of cow dung and ate it. When I reached home I thought that in no religious book is it written that an image of Lord Krishna or Rama has ever directed any disciple to eat cow dung. So I thought that it was not the real Krishna who had asked me to eat the cow dung. Because I am a Hindu, and I had been given this idea that the Lord takes birth in the human form time to time, thus I started praying to Him. I wept continuously for 24 hours crying out to God that I wanted to see Him in the form of a human being. After 24 hours a doctor was sent for and after examining me he said that I had gone mad. But that morning at 4:00 a.m. the image of my spiritual Father [Shiv Brat Lal] appeared to me while I was asleep. It made me believe that He was the incarnation of Lord Rama. Then I wrote to him a letter every week regularly for 10 months. After 10 months he wrote to me, "Faqir, I am receiving your letters. I admire your aspirations. I have realized Reality, Truth, Bliss and Peace in the fold of Radha Swami Faith from Rai Salig Ram Sahib."

Mark Juergensmeyer: Where was Maharishi Shiv Brat Lal at that time?

Faqir Chand: He was at Lahore at that time. But now he is dead. There is only a samadh [burial tomb] of his. I went to him in Lahore and he initiated me in the Path of the Radhaswami Faith. After about 10 years I went abroad in the First Great War. I remained there alone without my family, and I did a lot of sadhana as is written in our religious books. I saw the Light within and listened to the Sound as is written in the texts of the Radhaswami Faith. But I could not get peace, though I had happiness. You understand me? I got happiness; I got bliss; I got inward pleasure and I also got miraculous powers, but not peace. Then I used to worry my spiritual Father asking him to tell me about that thing on the authority of which Swami Ji and Kabir had condemned all religions. Because in the books of Radhaswami faith and by Kabir it is written that none except the Saints have realized the Reality. They have said that Rama and Krishna were the incarnations of universal mind and not of the Real God. These saints have further claimed that Muslims have also not reached there and the Christians too have not reached there. So I could not understand that religious philosophy. Once I come on annual leave from Iraq. I went to Hazur Data Dayal Ji Maharaj, my spiritual Father, and troubled him a lot with my love. I followed him everywhere like his shadow. At last he said, "See me tomorrow." Next day, when I went to him, he put one coconut and five [coins] in my lap and said, "I give you an order, obey me: The Real Master shall meet you in the form of your disciples." That is what my spiritual Father told me.

Mark Juergensmeyer: What stages or regions did you reach within according to the Radhasoami faith?

Faqir Chand: There are different stages, different colors and different sounds. I had seen all. But I was not satisfied with all this inward abhyas. So he gave me this work just to make me realize the Reality. When I came to this line as a guru or as a master my eyes were opened. Why? Because those who regard me as their guru and those who consider me as their master my image appears to them in their meditation, in their dreams and even in a state of wakefulness and guides them, whereas I remain unaware of all this. You understand me, what I am telling you? I want to be very frank with you. You have come for research. I am telling you my personal life. Daily I receive many letters. Some people write that I went there in an airplane to take

63

a dying man; some say that I come on a horse; and others write that I come in a palanquin at the time of the death of a man, whereas I do not go anywhere. All what they see in meditation, in dreams or in wakefulness, all proves to me that all what we see inside is nothing but subtle matter or illusion. I think you are following me.

Mark Juergensmeyer: Yes, I follow.

Faqir Chand: There is a student. He says that when he went to the examination hall for a science paper he did not know that difficult paper. He prayed to me. I appeared there, sat under the desk, and dictated the answers to those difficult questions. The student got 98 marks out of 100. The truth is that I myself do not know science, nor did I go to his examination hall. About five days ago a lady sent me two packs of apples and some other fruit, along with a letter that she was having her bath in a river in Kashmir. Suddenly a wave of water came and took her away for 10 or 15 yards. She writes that when she was drowning I appeared there, caught her hand, and brought her out of the river and said to her, "You have yet to do a lot of work." Now she writes to me in her letter to let her know as to what work she is to do? Now neither did I go there to save her, nor did I tell her that she has yet to do a lot of work. This is the secret which has been kept so guarded by all the religions and even by the gurus of the Radhaswami Faith. They have kept the public in dark. They have exploited us; they have robbed us; they have cheated us and they have deceived us by saying that they go, whereas they do not go or manifest themselves to anybody. They have admitted this truth before me. . . My own spiritual brother Bhai Nandu Singh agreed with me. Now he is dead and in his place Sri Anand Rao is working in Andhra Pradesh [Sri Anand Rao has since died]. So, from all these experiences, I have come to know that whatever we see in the form of our ideal [depends on our own karmic perspective]. If one's mind is pure then the answer that one would get from the manifested ideal shall be true. But if one's mind is not pure, then the answer will be wrong and there is every possibility that the ideal may put you on the wrong way of life if your mind is not pure.

Now, at this age, I meditate on light and sound. And I try to find out, who is seeing the light within and who is listening to the sound within. Sometimes after two or three months when I go into deep meditation my "Self" stands separated from the Light and Sound. There I lose my own entity. I forget who am I. I know nothing about God, I know nothing about my guru and I know nothing about my own self [ego]. From all such experience I have come to this conclusion that Who am I? I am a bubble of supermost consciousness. That is what my realization is. This is what I have gained. Now what I feel is that there is One, Infinite, Supermost Element. From it, when it moves, sound and light come out and from that light and sound this creation takes place. Cosmic rays and many other types of rays come out of this light and sound and all this gross matter is made. So it is the Will of that Supreme Power. Everything is oozing out of it and is merging back in it. There is egoism in us and it moves us to do this or to do that. There are four kinds of egoisms in us: 1. Egoism of Physical Form; 2. Egoism of Mental Form; 3. Egoism of Light Form; and, 4. Egoism of Sound Form. I ask myself, what have I attained? Silence in the beginning and silence in the end. Whatever is happening, it is all His Will. Every philosopher or saint who came and made inward search for realization wrote his experience. But their followers in order to gain fame and name and to collect wealth kept this a secret from the general public. Though to keep the secret was necessary in those days, it is not required now. Today humanity has been divided into different sects and religions. Every day there are communal conflicts in the world. Hindus and Muslims are fighting and Arabs and Jews are fighting. Therefore, after realizing the secret, I raised the slogan of Be Man. Why? My spiritual Father had told me, "Before leaving your physical frame change the teachings." So I have changed the teachings. No one on this earth, he may be Christ, he may be Radhaswami, he may be Kabir or he may be anybody--none has the right to say that he has understood the Reality in all respects. That power is bigger, bigger, bigger, bigger and bigger. Our senses cannot reach there. This is what I have understood. So I pass my life helping others, serving the poor and preaching the truth. I have three free hospitals here. To the general public I preach the art of living a happy life. You sleep and you enter the state of dream. In dream you feel angry with one. You hit him in the dream. Your hand in that state of dream is moved. You are frightened in your dream and you speak and your tongue is moved. You create a woman in your dream and you enjoy sex with her. Your semen is discharged. These are the effects of the thoughts of your dreams, which are not in your control. It proves that the thoughts of your mind are capable to have effect upon your body.

In the state of wakefulness we hate others and we keep enmity with others. All that we do in our state of wakefulness, with our own will, it must have its effect upon us. I have proven to you that if involuntary thoughts can effect our body, why not voluntary thoughts should have their effect upon us? So what I myself practice I advise others to adopt in their lives. Always be optimistic. Do not harm others for your personal benefit. Do not think ill of others. This is one thing which I preach. Secondly, if anybody wants that he should not come to this earth again in any form or in any other life, for such people I have [the exposed secret] with me.

Mark Juergensmeyer: What is that Truth?

Faqir Chand: When I am alone I ask myself, "What have you gained?" I have gained nothing and I have gained everything. I have got no desire to achieve now. Because I have realized that I am a bubble of super consciousness. That Supreme Power has created this Universe. Thoughts we take from outside and some bud out from within. Life is nothing but a dream. There is only one Truth, which is always one and only one. After this realization I have got Peace. Due to my past karmas I am still alive; I do not know how long that Power shall keep me in this body. I have a lone desire that after my death, if I get anywhere, I may be able to tell the world what happens to me after death. This is my only desire.

Mark Juergensmeyer: Where do you think you will go after death?

Faqir Chand: So far as my realization is concerned, bubble will merge in the ocean. Light will merge in the light. But whatever I have thought and whatever I have said that will remain in this Universe. Because matter is never destroyed. Whatever I am talking now, it shall remain in this room.

Mark Juergensmeyer: When you hear the purest sound and see the purest light, what color is that purest light?

Faqir Chand: That light is white. There are different colors and kinds of lights within. As the sun shines in the morning it looks red. In the evening when it sets we again see it red. It is due to clouds, dust and other particles that are in the sky which make us see the sun as red, otherwise sun is not red. It is all white. Similarly the red light of soul (atma) is white. Because we have desires they cover our souls and according to the desires of the worldly things the light is different.

Mark Juergensmeyer: The purest light is white?

Faqir Chand: I cannot say it was white. But I can say that it is more than white [as in a literal color].

Mark Juergensmeyer: And the sound?

Faqir Chand: Yes, sound, I used to listen [to] bells, thunders of cloud and veena. But now I listen only one Sound, which is an unbreakable tune, about which I cannot say any word. It is what it is. But what does it give to me? It gives peace and bliss. Now at this age of 92 years I do not care for the sound and light too. Why? Because light is seen by "Me" [Self] and sound is heard by "Me" [Self]. Then who is great? Light or sound or He who sees it and listens to it? Who is great? Light is great or "I" [as Transcendental Self] am great? Sound is great or I am great? The self of mine is the super most Element of consciousness in my body. If that is not there then sound is of no value and light is of no value to me. That is what I have realized. I do not know about myself, brother, what will be my end. You have come from America. Whatever I have realized I have told you.

Now, after having a long experience of my life, I feel that most of the past mahatmas and the present gurus by keeping the secret Truth unrevealed/undisclosed have been unfair to the public and have often exploited them. They have taken undue advantage of the ignorance of the people. They have built their own big buildings. They have made air-conditioned rooms for themselves. These gurus enjoy themselves and the poor people being ignorant give their hard earned money to these gurus at the cost of their comforts and those of their children. I do not deny I receive donations, but I personally do not use even a single penny out of these donations. My own son is well placed.

He draws about Rupees 2500 per month. He is a big metallurgist, Russia returned.

Mark Juergensmeyer: Yes, what does he do?

Faqir Chand: He is at Bhilai Steel Plant as a metalurgist. So I have my own means of earnings. Whatever is received here in the form of donation is spent for the ailing poor and on publications published by the Mandir. My publications are distributed gratis. Daily I receive a lot of mail and some people write that my form is seen by them and [a miracle has been done] for them. But I am ignorant of all that. Whatever sometimes I say to somebody comes out true, and he thinks that I have done it. But this is wrong. I have not done it.

Mark Juergensmeyer: Then should one have a guru?

Faqir Chand: Guru means Knowledge; without guru we cannot achieve anything. Our mother is our guru, our father is our guru, our friend is our guru and the world around us is our guru. But the Real Guru who makes the Self free from the bondage of this world is called the Sat Guru. And to attain the Reality the Sat Guru must be a perfect man. Nowadays this guruism has become a source of earning one's keep.

Mark Juergensmeyer: You know, some people say that science is also a guru.

Faqir Chand: Yes, science is also a teacher. But excuse me, unless someone is there to explain to you about it, you will not understand anything about it. Therefore, external guru is most essential and important. Although the knowledge is in the student, he cannot attain that knowledge without a teacher or a professor, who teaches him and makes him [come to] realize that knowledge which is within that student. But if the brain of the student is not capable and receptive then teacher or professor may do anything, he would not be able to understand it. Yes, anything else you want to ask?

Mark Juergensmeyer: Well, after you, will there be any other teacher?

Faqir Chand: I have no right to say anything about this subject, but I may tell you that where there is demand there is supply. It is the law of nature. When the public will face the troubles and when they will seek for peace, nature will create so many teachers. You know, there are different kinds of brains. If some accident occurs, some people rush to that place to rob the victims, some go there to give them food, some go there to give medical aid, some other goes there to know the cause of the accident and to thrash the person responsible for the accident, and still some other people go there to find out the ways and means so that such accidents may not occur again. The great brains come in this world as per the desires and the needs of mankind. All the great saints such as Mahavira and Buddha and others come according to the demand of the times. It is His will. I cannot say definitely, but this much I am certain that when there is too much heat nature automatically brings storms and rains. If it is too cold, then nature automatically brings heat.

It is a natural process about which He only knows. About me, there are so many miracles attributed to me that if I write about all there would be a big book. But I say upon my honor that I do none of these miracles. It is either fate or the faith of the person concerned. In case of some trouble my disciples remember me, my image appears to them and helps them and they write to me, whereas I do not know anything myself. So from all this I have realized that every man is perfect. Be true to your own self. That is what my religion is. Do not think or dream of harming anybody for your personal benefit. This is the only religion that I have to propagate; then have this belief that there is one Supreme Power. Believe Him in any form you love or like--Jesus Christ, Rama, Krishna, Faqir Chand or Baba Charan Singh or anybody else. But have faith in one. Neither [the saint] helps you nor Faqir Chand helps you. It is your own faith, your own desire that helps you. . . .

Well, my dear Mark, I do not know whether whatever I have realized is correct or incorrect. I do not claim that I am correct, but I have spent my life very purely. I have been true to my parents and I have been true to my officers.

I am a retired military man. What I have realized after a long search is that one must not think ill or do any harm to anybody for one's personal benefit. Second, one must have faith in only one form, it may be of any God, Goddess or a Guru. Without Form one cannot reach the goal. For instance, you have passion, unless you consider a lady as your wife you cannot enjoy your passions. If you have to satisfy your greed, unless you believe anything as gold or currency you cannot feel happy. Similarly about attachment. If you do not consider someone as your son or daughter, you cannot enjoy the feelings of attachment. So, if you want to reach that ultimate goal, you must have faith in one Form thinking him Perfect.

Therefore the worship of Christ, Rama, Krishna or Guru is most essential. In the beginning it is very essential. People think me to be a saint or realized man. Their belief makes them solve their own problems, whereas I am not even in the know of such things. It proves that everything is within you and not outside. The Radhaswami Faith, or the philosophy of saints, makes a man realize that everything is within you and not outside. I do not say that my search is final. Truth is not known to anybody. As you sow, so shall you reap. This is the law that governs this globe. Everything depends upon your own thinking.

Mark Juergensmeyer: Are there some other disciples of Swami Shiv Brat Lal?

Faqir Chand: Yes, there are a few.

Mark Juergensmeyer: Do they preach the same thing as you preach?

Faqir Chand: You see, the plane at which I speak everybody cannot speak. Why? Because I have got no attachment. I do not want respect, money or fame. This institution is a registered trust recognized by the government. Whatever anybody gives that is spent for the benefit of the public. Those gurus, who have personal interest, say things in different ways. My area is not too vast. Only the educated people come to me and those who have spent their life in meditation or sadhana. My teaching for beginners is not suitable. I know it. But I cannot now teach A.B.C. It is not in my power. Only the professors, teachers, doctors and judges come to me the most, because they understand what I say. Everyone of us is a bubble of consciousness. But there is egoism in it. Egoism of body, egoism of mind, egoism of soul and egoism of surat. When this egoism goes away what remains? Silence in the beginning and silence in the end. Pass your life cheerfully.

Mark Juergensmeyer: Do the women face any difficulty in realizing themselves?

Faqir Chand: This I cannot say. Ladies must know themselves. Very frank talk it is. They know better about their difficulties, but I may tell you one thing. He who indulges much in sex cannot realize Reality. This is my final research. This is what I told the Americans last time and this is what I shall tell them again.

Mark Juergensmeyer: That means there is no difficulty to women.

Faqir Chand: No, soul of woman and of man is the same. When it comes in the material form only then there is difference. Some soul comes in the form of a lady or wife and the other in the form of a man or a husband. The modern science is proving many old beliefs to be futile. The angle of understanding is now different. The present educated people and the scientists are not going to believe blindly the religion as we have been believing in the past. I am not afraid of anything while I speak the Truth. Last time when I went to America I delivered a lecture to about one thousand Americans in the Research Association called A.R.E. and told them: "You say that Jesus Christ was the son of God; it was not only Jesus Christ who was the son of God, we all are the sons of God." I further said that "In the Bible [it states that] the earth is flat, whereas the scientists have proved that the earth is round. The first scientist who proved this fact was hanged." When I was telling this my friend Dr. I.C. Sharma [now Faqir Chand's successor] pressed my feet, so that I might not speak the Truth. But I said that was Truth, why should I not speak it?

Even our Lord Krishna, who is believed to be the incarnation of God among Hindus, lost all his children and grandchildren before his very eyes, fighting against one another after drinking wine. What could Krishna do? Every man must reap the fruit of his own deeds. He may be a prophet, a saint or anybody. Even these incarnations have not been free from sufferings for their own action. Even some very great men died a miserable death. I do not know about myself, how would I die. Though at this age of 92 years I am better than many. My spiritual Father had asked me to change the teachings. I do not know what should I change. He never told me to raise the voice of Be Man. He never told me

71

to open this Library. He simply said to me, "Change the teachings." So, whatever I have realized, if someone cares for it, let him care, and if somebody does not care let him not. If someone wants to read my books, let him read. I do not care. If somebody wants to give some donation here for the help of the poor, let him give, and if somebody does not give, let him not. I have my own means of livelihood. I have my own home to live in.

Last time I was sick for some days and then I remained here in this room. When I went home I paid 45 rupees to the Mandir as a rent of this room. I might be wrong my friend. It is possible, but my conscience is clear. I am True to my "Self." In other ashrams people take service from the disciples for gardening and other odd jobs. But I never get such work here from anyone. If somebody wants to do any service willingly, let him do it. But I do not want to ask anybody.

Mark Juergensmeyer: There is a framed letter from Virginia. Do they proclaim you as their guru?

Faqir Chand: Yes, they love me dearly.

Mark Juergensmeyer: But you do not want to be a guru?

Faqir Chand: I have never initiated people as others do. Whatever I say in my discourses is the only "Nam" or initiation. Those who believe me take my hints and act upon them. They are benefited. If anyone with sincere heart comes to me with any desire, I wish that his desire be fulfilled.

Mark Juergensmeyer: What is the significance of the word Radhaswami?

Faqir Chand: Radha is our Real Self; Swami is that place from where it has oozed out. Radha is Real Self, which is neither body, nor mind, neither light nor sound. To take that Self back to its origin and the state of reunion of Self with its Origin is called Radhaswami, this is what I have understood.

Mark Juergensmeyer: For meditation, is this word a mantra?

72

Faqir Chand: First one must undertake such meditation as may take the meditator away from the physical senses. This practice is known as the repetition of Nam given by the master to his disciple. So by repeating that Nam, not with tongue but with mind, here amidst the eyebrows, you go above the physical senses, as you go above in the dream while sleeping. Then comes the mental region, from where the thoughts ooze out. As the process of thinking starts, different kinds of pictures and scenes come before us. To surpass them or to go beyond the mental region and its creations, you are to undertake the practice of dhyan of the master. We people [have a tendency to fall asleep and dream] by this practice, but by concentrating on the face of a guru, provided one thinks him as the real master and Perfect, then the mental senses will also cease, or the meditator shall not have any feeling of mental existence as well.

Beyond this is the Light. The entity which lives in the Light, sees the Light and enjoys the bliss of Light is our Soul or Atma. Beyond that is Sound or Shabd. When one listens to that Sound one forgets all about the first three stages that [comprises a trinity]: body, mind and light. That is the 4th stage according to the saints. But I have realized the 5th stage too. Reference to 5th stage is also made by Saint Kabir in his writings. But that cannot be understood by everybody. The 5th stage is that condition where one loses one's entity as an individual. Self merges in the Supreme as a drop mingles in the ocean. So far I have not been able to merge myself in that 5th stage. I try my best, but I fail. Why? I do not know. Therefore, I say that it is not in man's hands to reach that stage. It is either His Will or the destiny of a man. So, at this age of 92, I surrender myself to that Supreme One.

The Secret

ॐ

ज़प्ति

The Secret

One

I do not know whether my realizations are right or wrong. I do not make any claim that my realization is final. People say that my form manifests to them and helps them in solving their worldly as well as mental problems, but I do not go anywhere nor do I know anything about such miraculous instances. At Sarsonheri a person came to me. He had suffered from a paralytic attack. Now he was able to walk, but still the paralytic attack had left its effect on his left side. However, he was not suffering from any serious trouble. He was an old man and a widower. His daughter, who accompanied him, told me that when her father suffered from the attack she prayed to me. I appeared there and told her that her father would be all right. She said to her father, "Baba Ji has come and says that you would be all right." Her father said that he did not see Baba Ji anywhere. Then his daughter directed him to see straight in front, and thus he also saw my form standing there. That man told me that I remained with him for twenty-two days, until he was well. What is this?

Two

I am here not forever. Death must come one day. For what should I spoil my true self? When I adopted this path of life, I had pledged that I would follow this path with Truth and shall speak to the world my realization of this path. The writings did not reveal the Truth to me. Denunciations of my forefathers in the writings of the Saints pained me, but I had a firm faith in His Holiness Hazur Data Dayal Ji Maharaj. His Holiness had directed me, "Faqir, change the mode of preaching before abandoning this mortal frame."

Now, after having such experiences with me, I question myself, "Faqir Chand, say, what mode of preaching do you wish to change? Which teachings should I change?" The change that I can make in the present mode of preaching I explained in the discourses that I delivered during my tour. The change is, "O man, your real helper is your own Self and your own Faith, but you are badly mistaken and believe that somebody from without comes to help you. No Hazrat Mohammed, no Lord Rama, Lord Krishna or any God or goddess or Guru comes from without. This entire game is that of your impressions and suggestions which are ingrained upon your mind through your eyes and ears and of your Faith and Belief." This is the change that I am ordained to bring about.

Three

Shri Jagan Nath is present here. He offered me 403 rupees for the Manavta Mandir. He told [me] that I awakened him at 1:30 A.M. a day before. But I did not go to awake him nor do I know anything about it. Possibly other mahatmas and gurus might have the knowledge of such instances of manifestations of their forms. At least I remain unaware. Many of the present gurus have admitted before me that they remain unaware about such instances. His Holiness Data Dayal Ji also said in his last discourses that he did not go anywhere, but he did not disclose this Truth in his early discourses. My entire life and my mission is based upon Truth. My realization and research is ahead of the realizations and research of the previous Saints. I have not followed their trodden path of maintaining an iron curtain around the Truth. They kept mankind in the dark. The great Saints of the past suffered from untold miseries in their lives perhaps due to this very reason.

The question is why these great Saints suffered? I have my suspicion that these Saints suffered because they did not speak out the total Truth to the world. The cause of their sufferings might be their untruthful living. I am myself not aware of my own end. I feel pained when I contemplate upon the miserable end of the great Saints. I am not here forever. For what should I indulge in deceitful acts? To me, my "Self" is more dear than anything else in the world; therefore, I always speak the plain truth - that I do not manifest anywhere, nor am I aware of my manifestation to any person at any place. Some people said at the time of their death that Baba Ji had come in an airplane to take them along. Others said that Baba Ji had brought a horse and others said that Baba Ji had come in a palanquin. But I do not know anything about such instances. I simply wonder when people narrate to me such instances of their near and dear ones. I fearlessly proclaim and appeal to the present gurus of the religious world that either they should contradict what I say, or they should speak out the truth that they too do not manifest themselves to their respective devotees. If they too are sailing in the same boat in which I sail, then why do they keep their poor devotees in the dark and exploit them?

Four

In obedience to the dictates of His Holiness Hazur Data Dayal Ji wherever I went during this tour I said, "O man, be Pure in your deed and be Pure in your conscience." When these great Saints, who spent their lives in meditation, could not save themselves from the fruit of their deeds, then how can you householders be an exception? You cherish enmity against your brothers for selfish gains; you oppose and fight against your parents and you do not hesitate in deceiving your friends. You yourself decide, how would you save yourself? You study your own life and examine what you do. We pray for the death of our own real brother, so that we may inherit his property as well. We indulge in litigation against our parents, brothers and sisters for more and more property. Wives go to the court of law against their husbands and husbands against their wives. How can such people aspire for higher values of life and live happily?

Five

Nowadays this phenomena of manifestations is the main cause of religious exploitation of the ignorant devotees. This is the root of communal rivalries. Recently in Benares it led to communal riots between Hindus and Muslims. Benares remained under curfew for a week. Why? Because both Hindus and Muslims are ignorant of the Truth.

In this age of machine Saints incarnate to reveal the Truth, but unfortunately whatever the great Saints like Guru Nanak, Kabir and Radha Swami Dayal have said their devotees do not adopt it in their lives. Their sayings and teachings are used as tools for gaining personal name, fame and wealth by the present gurus and preachers. Ignorant masses are advised to get initiated, for they shall be led to heavens by their guru after their death. Had many of the present gurus not confessed to me that they too remain unaware about their manifestation I would have thought that I am in the wrong. The late Bhai Nandu Singh Ji of

Nizamabad, Shri Anand Rao Ji of Secundrabad and Sant Tara Chand Ji have admitted that they too do not manifest themselves to their respective disciples. Of late another Guru known as Shehan-Shah, who works as successor to Sant Kirpal Singh Ji in the Western countries, met me in the train at Sonepat Railway Station. He is a friend of Pir Mughan Sahib. He also admitted that his form also manifests to his devotees, but he does not know anything about his manifestations. Unfortunately none of them speaks out the Truth on the platform.

Six

I tell you an incident of my own life. My daughter Prem Piari was married for some years, but she had no child. Once my daughter and her husband went to Firozpur in connection with a marriage in the family of Pandi Wali Ram. My daughter came to me and complained that her mother-in-law and other members of the family taunt her and trouble her for being childless even after five years of married life. I consoled her saying, "Daughter! you are born to a Faqir, why bother about children and suffer pains? What is the surety of life, for what should you have a desire for children? Do not listen to others and remain busy with your own work.

She went away and after about ten minutes, Shri Des Raj, my son-in-law, came and he also complained about the necessity of a child. I promptly said, "Why do you worry about this? You shall have many children." This thought never struck my mind that why I have made two different statements to my daughter and son-in-law on the same subject? Neither could I ever think that my daughter would die. As preordained, my daughter and son-in-law went in for a second marriage and now he is a father of many children.

What I wish to convey by narrating this incident is that a Saint speaks or tells only that which is destined to happen. No Saint can cancel the result of your deeds. What is allotted cannot be blotted. The punishment for his or her deeds can be minimized by those who understand this and then act upon what a Saint says. Simple initiation into a particular religious sect would not serve your purpose. It would not save you from the result of your bad deeds. This is the plain Truth that I am explaining to you. If you like, you may come and listen to me. If you don't, you may not. You may give any donation to the

Mandir or not; you may read any book of mine or not. At least I do not want to spoil my "Self."

Seven

During this tour I also visited the Ashram of Sant Tara Chand Ji at Dinod in Haryana state. About ten years ago he had come to me at Delhi. He had thought that if Baba were a Saint he would give me his left-out food. He came and sat among others. He had no distinct clothing, nor did I know him. In the meantime a cup of tea came for me. I took about two or three sips, and then handed over the cup to Shri Tara Chand saying, "Get to work; you shall be well known in the world." What was this? I did not say anything intentionally to Tara Chand. It was destined to happen.

Now I went to his Ashram, which is double of our Manavta Mandir. There are very big halls. There are provisions to serve food to at least one thousand people in stainless steel utensils. Tara Chand thinks that this is all the fruit of my blessings. Now, I think that whatever was said by me to Sant Tara Chand, it was pre-destined for him. If my blessings can help in establishing bigger centers than my own then why should not I give the same blessings to all who come to me? It is the law of thought radiation that works. When he came his thought radiations touched my mind and I involuntarily said what was due to happen.

On the basis of such experiences I say that no Saint can give you anything. A Saint speaks out only that which is to happen. This is what I have understood. I do not know anything about others. I may be wrong. I do not make any high claims. If a Saint can give you anything at all, it is the true knowledge of going beyond the ocean of existence. He can tell you the art of living a happy and contented life. This is all that a Saint can do. This is what I have realized after a long search.

Eight

Different people from different walks of life come to me for blessings. Sometimes I say something and sometimes I do not say anything. Some time back, a man from Hyderabad sent a draft of 10,000 Rupees to the Mandir, with a condition that he should recover from his illness. I did not accept that draft for the

Mandir, but deposited it in the name of the sender and wrote to him that life and death were not in my hands. . . My inner self did not accept that donation. Thus, I did not allow that draft to be credited to the Mandir account.

I did not receive any news from that man for about one and a half months. Now I have received a letter from his wife that her husband is dead, and that the money her husband had sent to the Mandir may be returned to her. I returned that amount to her. Now the question is why did I not write to that man that he shall recover from his illness? To others, who come for such blessings, I do say so. Why, to that man, did I hesitate? What is to happen must happen.

When I reached Dinod (ashram of Sant Tara Chand Ji), a young man came there and said to me, "What is your name? From where have you come and why have you come here?" I thought him a man of the C.I.D. But later I learned that he was a journalist. I told him that I was a Faqir; I had come from Hoshiarpur to bow my head at the hallowed feet of my Sat Guru Dev Sant Tara Chand Ji. He further enquired, "Is Tara Chand Ji your Guru? How is he your Guru?" I told him that just as Swami Virjanand was the Guru of Swami Dayanand, but the sublime Truth was revealed to Dayanand Ji by the statue of Lord Shiva, similarly I attained the Sublime Knowledge from Sant Tara Chand Ji and my other such disciples. Thus I have come here to pay my respects to Tara Chand Ji, a True Form of my Sat Guru.

Nine

If thou hast sustained life, impart Sat Guru's True Name!
By imparting the True Name, thou shalt attain peace!

See what golden words are written, that if you have come in human body then impart the True Name of Sat Guru. By doing so, what shall you gain? Peace. I have attained Peace. Why did I go to Sant Tara Chand Ji? Why do I respect Dayal Dass Ji? Why do I have regards for Kamalpur Wali Mata (old lady disciple of Kamalpur)? Why did I bow my head to Shri Krishak Ji? Because from them I have attained Peace. How did I gain this Peace from them? When they told me that my form manifested to them and directed them to the highest stages of spirituality within but without any knowledge of mine then I was obliged to realize that whatever forms or scenes I used to visualize within were nothing but mere projections of my mental impressions and feelings. All those inner scenes, colors and forms that I used to visualize and enjoy proved a mere fancy and illusion, thus I attained Peace. I attained the true knowledge of dwelling in my own "Self."

Ten

At Dinod people offered me about 1000 rupees which I handed over to Sant Tara Chand Ji. I had no right to accept that amount from the poor people, though I accepted an amount of 1600 rupees from Shri Tara Chand. Sant Tara Chand told me that I had helped him in reaping his crop of grams. Other people also narrate such instances, but I do not go anywhere. I did not initiate them, but they believe that I am their Guru. Their belief in me has helped me to realize the Truth. What Truth? The Truth is that all these manifestations of Guru, God, Goddess, Rama or Krishna are not a Reality, but an illusion. I am convinced of this Truth. With this realization I have attained Peace. The root cause of disquietude is mind. Once its real form is recognized, you attain Peace. I have recognized the real form of my mind. Sant Kabir writes:

Disciple bows to the Guru, tis known to all!
Guru bows to the disciple, tis very rare!

This is the secret of Sant Mat (belief of the Saints) which was kept intact behind the iron curtain of gurudom. I have removed this curtain. His Holiness Swami Ji Maharaj revealed this secret through symbols. Once one disciple said to Swami Ji, "Rai Saligram Sahib is your great devotee and true disciple." His Holiness replied, "Who knows whether Salig Ram is my Guru or I am his."

Similarly Hazur Data Dayal Ji Maharaj used to say about me. Whenever I visited His Holiness at Lahore, He used to say in his discourses, "This Faqir has come to enlighten me and to lead me beyond the Phantasmagoria."

This secret has caused a great harm to mankind. We householders have been befooled by the so called gurus. Our hard earnings have been taken away by them and even then they expect that we should remain in their very circle ever bowing to their feet. Many people come and prostrate before me as well.

Why? Because they are not aware of the Truth. They are ignorant of the Secret. I often say that I have come from the Anami Dham, the Nameless Abode, to tell that "O man, know thyself by thyself."

There is no difference between you and a Guru. But you are ignorant and you are very much governed by your mind. You run after the gurus and sadhus for the fulfillment of your worldly desires. You make humble entreaties to the gurus. When these gurus themselves have disobedient and characterless children, and when they themselves do not have good relations with their wives, how do you think that they would do any good to you? Therefore, I again emphasize my point, "O man! your good lies in your own deeds." A True Guru simply reveals to you the secret or the Truth. The Truth is that this world is a field of the deeds. Whatever deeds you or I have done, we must face their results. No power on earth can protect us. This is the Truth.

Eleven

Sometimes I think that whatever I have understood so far may be wrong. But I do not repent because my conscience is very clear. I have never said or done anything for any selfish motive. I never throw dust in your eyes to get name or fame for this short life. This is also a fact - that I need money for Manavta Mandir - but I never wish to adopt fraudulent methods for the collection of money. If anybody wishes to help the Mandir happily, he may, but if one does not want then one may not. I care not for the position of a preceptor. I have fear and my life trembles at the thought of the harvest of bad deeds, for we all must reap the harvest of our deeds. If you live upon the hard earnings of others, you deceive others and you indulge in acts of fraud for your selfish motives. Then where would you go? Who would save you when great Saints themselves could not remain safe? O! my Preceptor, I do not know whether I am right or wrong. I challenge all the Saints and gurus of the present to denounce me if I am wrong. I shall not mind. I only tell what has happened or is happening with me.

Twelve

When I went to Dinod I sincerely thought - did I go to reap the crops of Tara Chand? No, not at all. I did not know anything about it until Tara Chand Ji told me. Now Tara Chand says that if Baba Ji had not come his way he would have become an egotist. Whatever form manifests to you it is the form of your own faith and belief. But we are divided into different religions and sects on the basis of these very manifestations. O! householders I have come for you. Do not be misled by any false promises. Try to understand the Truth and purify your deeds. Open you eyes, Jagan Nath, I did not go to awaken you at 1:30 a.m., day before yesterday. I did not even know about you earlier. You have donated four hundred rupees. I do need money for the Mandir. I express my thanks to you, but I speak the Truth. You may accept it or not. I have done my duty towards you. If what I have experienced in life has been the experience of other gurus and Saints, then I would say these gurus, whosoever they be, did not do anything good to us. They befooled us, exploited us and looted us for their own name, fame and for establishing their religious estates.

Thirteen

How does one attain peace? How did I gain peace? I can tell about that alone. When Krishak Ji came he handed me his diary in which he had written in detail about how my form guided him in his inner search from time to time. I put one coconut and five paisa at his feet and bowed to him. I permitted him to initiate the aspirants saying, "You would yourself realize the Truth." He stayed in the Mandir for about ten months. I paid eighty rupees for his expenses and sixty rupees to his attendant, because he helped me to attain peace. I did not initiate Dayal Dass nor did I impart Nam to Kamalpur Wali Mata. It was their faith and belief that helped them. They accepted my word as Nam and me as their Guru. But I gained the more. My entire struggle and search for the Guru came to an end. I recognized my mind and attained Peace. Now my practice starts beyond the regions of mind i.e., from the Light. The philosophy of Radhasoami faith also directs that the aspirant should go beyond mental regions to Satya-Lok. Only then liberation would be achieved.

Fourteen

He who gives them [love, affection, and belief] to others gains himself. So, it is the belief of the people that benefits them. I do not do anything. Their faith and belief in me brings their cherished fruit to them. It is not "I" who manifests myself to them.

To give love and affection to others means to have faith in them, to believe them. I too have benefited from this. I daily receive a number of letters in which people write, "Baba Ji, by contemplating upon your holy form, we achieved this thing and our difficult problems were solved." I do nothing. It is their own love and affection that fructifies. Therefore I say that whomsoever you believe have firm faith that He is Perfect, Sublime, and Omnipotent; all your problems shall be solved and all your works would be done. He who does not attend my discourses or listens to me in person, but contemplates upon forms, he worships the dead Guru. You do not understand the true meaning of Guru's worship. You consider that offering of money to the Guru and bowing at his feet is Guru worship. These are worldly customs and norms of our civilization. Those who simply contemplate upon the form of the Guru, they worship their own mind, because inner visions are the creations of your own mind, and nothing comes from without. This is what I have understood.

I know that I am speaking of things of a very high level, but I am helpless. Old men do not talk like small children. I am obliged to speak about that condition alone in which I dwell. People come to me, I speak to them with a very clean heart and sincere conscience. It is possible that I may be wrong. I have known the miserable end of the gurus and the Saints. I feel afraid. I do not know how I shall die, but if I also meet a miserable end and I remain conscious at the time of parting from this body then I shall also proclaim like Alexander the Great who said, "Keep my empty hands out of my coffin." I shall say that none should speak the Truth in this world, none should be sincere and none should live an honest life, but live as per one's desires!

Fifteen

I wonder when I study the lives of these Saints and mahatmas and doubt whether these mahatmas did any justice to their ignorant disciples. They did not disclose the total Truth as they knew it, possibly due to the paucity of true seekers or due to their selfish motives of name, fame and wealth. But if a disciple does not feel indebted to the Guru who imparts him True Knowledge then that disciple is most ungrateful.

I proclaim that I do nothing. Not just I, no one can do anything. Had anybody been able to do anything then these Saints must have, first of all, set their own children and wives on the right Path. Had Data Dayal Ji got any miraculous power he would not have allowed the disintegration of his own Dham (centre). I had predicted in 1919 to Hazur Data Dayal Ji that his centre would totter in ruins. Why did I say so? Because I had an insight. . . .

You come to me [and] I feel my responsibility and thus I speak the Truth to you without any reservation. I do not do any favour to you. Whatever I do, it is in obedience to the commands of Hazur Data Dayal Ji and Hazur Sawan Singh Ji Maharaj. Hazur Baba Sawan Singh Ji had said to me, "Faqir, carry on your work without any fear. I shall stand by you." Thus [I] speak the Truth without any fear, that everybody is bound to reap the fruit of his or her deeds. Do not live in this hope that you, a follower of Radhasoami, are initiated by a great Guru or that you are a devotee of Lord Krishna or Rama and thus you shall go free. Nay. Whatever deeds you do, fruit of those, must be reaped by you.

Sixteen

You must have read or listened to the story of Mahabharata. Arjuna achieved an impossible victory with the blessings of Lord Krishna. His power was unsurpassed and his arrows were irresistible. When the whole tribe of Lord Krishna died in civil war after Lord Krishna's death, Arjuna accompanied the remaining women and gopis to a safer place, but on the way the Bhils snatched away all the beloved wives of Lord Krishna from Arjuna. The unsurpassing strength and irresistible arrows of Arjuna could not protect those ladies of Lord Krishna's clan. This is the philosophy of karma. Who is safe and free from it? Whatever happens to us is all due to our own deeds. So why make a hue and cry when there is any distress for you? Why do you run hither and thither, weeping and pleading? Therefore I say time and again, "O! man you reform your ways and be clear in your conscience."

Perform your duty with compassion, remain detached from the world, recognize every creature like thyself, and attain the imperishable. Unless you attain to such a practical living, you can never get released from the cycle of transmigration, even though you might be initiated by a great Guru.

Many a time I question myself, "Faqir Chand, might you be endowed with some Supreme Power about which you may be ignorant?" For example, a beautiful lady goes through a bazaar, a young man looks at her and his mind is disturbed, but that woman remains ignorant of the mental condition of that man. If she could know the intentions of that man, she would positively give him a shoe beating. So, if nature has endowed me with *Something*, then why should I feel proud of it? It is the gift of Nature of which I can be deprived any time. It is His Will.

Patanjali, the great sage, has written in his book on Yoga that if you cannot do any inward practice then at least contemplate on the holy form of a Perfect Man. Now the question is, where would you search for a Perfect Man? I say that wherever or in whomsoever you have faith think that He is a Perfect Man and Omnipotent [and] your purpose shall be served. If my form manifests itself and helps those who have faith in me, then the form of other gurus also manifest themselves to their disciples and helps them. Leave aside the Saints, you put a wicked and immoral person on the seat of a Guru, develop faith in him, his form too shall manifest and help you like the manifested form of the great Saints. You are not helped by any Saint or Guru, but by your own faith and belief.

Seventeen

I question myself, "Faqir, have you gone astray? Are you misleading the world? Suppose I am wrong?" I do not feel guilty, because my conscience is clear and I have no selfish motive. If at all I am wrong then the responsibility lies upon the shoulders of Hazur Baba Sawan Singh and Hazur Data Dayal Ji. Why did they ask me to do this work? They were great Saints and had a great insight. Did they not know that I would speak the Truth? You will question me, as to why I have also asked some people to do this work of Satsang. I have given this work to them so that they may realize the Truth and their doubts and whims may vanish. I put Kamalpur Wali Mai as the Guru of women. Now her form manifests itself to many women, and she says that she does not know anything about the manifestation of her form. From such instances, if she realizes the Truth, she will attain Peace. Similarly, I asked Dayal Dass to work for his own realization and not for exploiting the innocent people and for deceiving the poor disciples.

People come to me with high hopes. I ask myself, "Why have you woven a spider's web? What good can you do to them?" The fact is that none is ready to receive the Knowledge that I wish to impart. I wish to show you that Path by following which you can attain liberation from the cycle of Transmigration. But you do not feel its necessity; you do not recognize its value. You come to me for solutions of your various social and worldly problems. Someone is unhappy with his wife; some other person is unhappy due to children. Some come for blessings to get a son, and some others come for the fulfillment of other worldly desires. Do you ever think about the reality of this world? Our existence in this world is not eternal. We are bound to leave this world, our beloved belongings and our kith and kin. Then why to clamor and weep for them? You will surely get your due. Live happily and peacefully.

Eighteen

Live a happy life and do not spend more than your income. Do not make offerings beyond your capacity. Do not cut short the necessities of your children to make donations to Manavta Mandir or to any other Guru and his centre. This would be the greatest sin on your part. Another thing for having a happy life is regular meditational practice without any break. It should be a part of your daily routine like eating and sleeping. Also make daily offerings of one thing or the other. Do you know what our forefathers used to do? They used to keep separate morsels for cow, dog and the crow before taking their meals. It was their Dharma not to eat without sharing their food with cow, dog and the crow. Do we follow their traditions? If you cannot offer any money in lump sum, try to save daily one paisa or two for offering to the needy or the destitute. This will inculcate in you a habit of sharing the offerings. If a man gives one lakh rupees in charity today, but does not give anything for years together, it would not benefit him as much as a man who makes daily offerings in one form or other. So adopt this principle of making daily offerings, to have daily meditation and to entertain daily new and constructive thoughts. These will help in transforming your life. He who gives in charity, his heart and mind become liberal and generous.

If you are economically not well off, you need not make offerings of money. Ladies, before cooking meals for the family, should keep one handful of flour or rice separately. After a week's accumulation of rice or flour, they should make chapattis of that flour or cook the rice and offer it to sparrows, dogs and the crows. I am telling these golden principles from the core of my heart. They seem to be very ordinary things. But do not consider them ordinary. These are principles for attaining a happy and prosperous life. Follow the above routine for all the 365 days of a year, and if your poverty still remains then do not offer flowers to my photograph but give any ill treatment that you can. Our sages were very wise. They knew the root cause of everything. But today we have totally ignored the traditions laid down by them. You try to understand the importance of old ceremonies and social practices. You do one good work a day and see how many good works would be to your credit after a year.

Inner Visions and Running Trains

One of the most remarkable aspects about the *Tibetan Book of the Dead* (or, more accurately speaking, The *Bardo Thotrol*) [1] is the principle that whatever one perceives during the dying process is ultimately illusory. Experiences of seeing inner light, hearing wondrous melodies, and feeling sensations of being out of the body, according to The *Bardo Thotrol*, are but momentary reflections of one's own psychological condition. As such, they are not to be valued in and of themselves, since they cannot by their nature reveal the ultimate truth, but only -- even if magnificently -- obscure it.

The reason for this is simple, if profound: whatever one sees in the dying process is a projection from one's owns self. Since this self/soul/ego in Buddhism is the root cause of man's suffering, and not a real and permanent condition, anything that reinforces, glamorizes, or even elevates its status is misleading and generative of delusion. The key to enlightenment in Mahayana Buddhism, unlike Christianity, is not salvation of the soul, but rather its annihilation as a continued sensation. Therefore, The *Tibetan Book of the Dead* is a practical text on how to carry out the process of death to its terminal apex: extermination of the individual self. At first glance this may seem a bit extreme, especially to those steeped in Western religions which place a higher value on personal immortality, but in light of Buddha's teachings it is perfectly consistent with his philosophy which views death -- real death -- in a very positive light.

What is perhaps most intriguing about the *Tibetan Book of the Dead*, at least from a scientific perspective, is its thoroughly rational and skeptical character. Although the text does instruct the neophyte to accept the clear void light as one's own, it does not describe in precise terms what that light is. Instead, it concentrates on what the light is not. It is not anything which can be seen, heard, touched or felt -- even on a higher or more elevated plane of awareness. It is, on the contrary, the suchness or context or spectrum out of which all things operate, but in and of itself cannot be grasped as any particular thing. Thus it is always identified through negation (neti, neti; "not this, not that") or through negative images: emptiness, void, vacuity, etc. It is, if we can describe it at all, no-thing.

The implications for the dying lama are clear: Do not accept whatever may arise in the intermediate stage just after death, for each apparition betrays its real origin, imputing a sense of reality and permanence upon something which has neither. Realize, rather, that nirvana is the source from which all visions arise and is therefore itself not a vision. Or, put in more philosophical terms, truth is the condition from which all conditions arise -- itself not being a secondary effect.

Surprisingly, one of the more lucid insights on the philosophy of the *Tibetan Book of the Dead* comes from a Hindu mystic, named Baba Faqir Chand, who apparently was not familiar with the original Tibetan text or its English translation. Although Faqir was not conversant with the *Bardo Thotrol*, he was nevertheless steeped in its philosophy as taught to him by his guru, Shiv Brat Lal of Gopiganj. Faqir Chand, like his lama counterparts, spent much of his life in meditation, attempting to consciously go through the dying process in order to prepare himself for his final exit. However, unlike others of his kind, Faqir left a detailed account of his some seventy plus years of meditation (ranging from 3 to 12 hours daily) which led up to his enlightenment. The result is a richly detailed account which provides a thorough understanding of how inner visions and the like are projected in the intermediate stages between life and death.

"As the *Bardo Thodol* [sic] text makes very clear by repeated assertions, none of all these deities or spiritual beings has any real individual existence any more than have human beings. "It is quite sufficient for thee (i.e., the deceased percipient) to know that these apparitions are (the reflections of) thine own thought-forms." They are merely the consciousness- content visualized, by karmic agency, as apparitional appearances in the Intermediate state -- airy nothings woven into dreams." --*Tibetan Book of the Dead* [2]

"Now, you see no Jesus Christ comes from without in anybody's visions. No Rama, no Krishna, no Buddha, and no Baba Faqir comes from without to anybody. The visions are only because of the impressions and suggestions that a disciple has already accepted in his mind. These impressions and suggestions appear to him like a dream. No body comes from without. This is the plain truth." --Baba Faqir Chand [3]

What strikes the reader almost immediately after reading both the *Bardo Thotrol* and *The Unknowing Sage* is the remarkable similarity between both texts. Whereas the *Bardo Thotrol* is written mostly in second person and third person, listing instructions for the departing soul, The Unknowing Sage is in first person, presenting the reader with Faqir Chand's frank autobiographical admissions about his meditative life. Yet, in both texts the respective philosophies coincide: 1) the illusory nature of religious visions; 2) the limitations of knowledge, both rational and transmundane; and 3) the principle that the ego/self/soul is the real cause of man's unenlightened state.

How Faqir Chand came to this realization is an interesting story in itself, especially for someone steeped in the Radhasoami tradition. From a very early age, Faqir was prone towards mystical experiences, oftentimes seeing religious visions of Krishna and Rama, who would, we are told, instruct Faqir on various aspects of his religious life. Eventually, however, Faqir became so distraught in his quest for God-Realization that he became hysterical and stopped eating. As Faqir recollects:

"Once I wept for twenty-four hours continuously for a glimpse of the Lord. Doctors were called in. They administered medicine to me. At about five o'clock in the morning I saw in a vision the form of Maharishi Shiv Brat Lal [Faqir's eventual guru]. He drew water from a nearby well and helped me take a bath, and then told me his address in Lahore. This experience convinced me that God had incarnated Himself in the form of Maharishi Shiv Brat Lal. " [4]

Faqir's experience convinced him that Shiv Brat Lal was an incarnation of the Lord. After ten months of correspondence, Faqir received initiation from his preceptor into the Radhasoami faith in 1905. [5] It was not until the end of World War One, though, that Faqir received his first glimpse of enlightenment. For prior to this time (1919), Faqir accepted whatever inner sights and sounds he beheld in meditation as true and objective. The turning point came after a battle in Hamidia in Iraq. Working as an inspector for the railway station, Faqir and his group came under heavy enemy attack. Fearing for his life, Faqir prayed internally for help from his guru, Shiv Brat Lal. Almost miraculously, Shiv Brat Lal appeared to Faqir in his inner vision. As Faqir recalls:

"I too was shaken with the fear of death. In this very moment of fear, the Holy Form of Hazur Data Dayal Ji appeared before me and said, "Faqir, worry not, the enemy has not come to attack but to take away their dead. Let them do that. Don't waste your ammunition." I sent for the Subedar Major and told him about the appearance of my Guru and his directions concerning the enemy. The Subedar Major followed the directions of my Guru. The rebel Jawans came and carried away their dead without attacking our positions. By six o'clock in the morning, our airplanes came and they dropped the necessary supplies. Our fears vanished. We gained courage. We were safe." [6]

Though Faqir was overjoyed by this miracle, he did not appreciate its full import until some three months later when he realized that it was a projection of his own mind. When Faqir asked Shiv Brat Lal about his appearance, the guru said that he knew nothing whatsoever about it. Moreover, around the time Faqir saw the miraculous form of his guru, Faqir's friends were also in danger and prayed to God. But instead of Shiv Brat Lal appearing to them, Faqir Chand's radiant form manifested and saved their lives. When Faqir was informed about this incident he was "wonder struck":

"After about three months, the fighting came to an end and the Jawans retired to their barracks. I returned to Bagdad, where there were many satsangis. When they learned of my arrival, they all came together to see me. It was all very unexpected and a surprising scene for me. I asked them, "Our Guru Maharaj is at Lahore. I am not your Guru. Why do you worship me?" They replied in unison, "On the battle field we were in danger. Death lurked over our heads. You appeared before us in those moments of danger and gave us direction for our safety. We followed your instructions and thus were saved." I was wonder struck by this surprising explanation of theirs. I had no knowledge of their trouble. I, myself, being in danger those days of combat, had not even remembered them. " [7]

Thus, it was through a series of remarkable events that Faqir began to question the authenticity of his inner visions. Instead of accepting whatever appeared to him during his voyages out of the body Faqir doubted them and attempted to find the source from which all such visions arise. Faqir's adventures began to dovetail at this point with the underlying philosophy of the *Bardo Thotrol*: "That all phenomena are transitory, are illusionary, are unreal, and non-existent save in the sangsaric mind perceiving them. . . That in reality there are no such beings anywhere as gods, or demons, or spirits, or sentient creatures --

all alike being phenomena dependent upon a cause. . . That this cause is a yearning or a thirsting after sensation, after the unstable sangsaric existence." [8]

Eventually, Faqir dismissed his visionary encounters as nothing but subtle obstructions of maya. It was at this point that Faqir's meditation took a new turn: instead of enjoying the bliss of inner sights and sounds, Faqir turned his attention to the source from which these manifestations arose. And in so doing, Faqir no longer became attracted to visions of Krishna, Rama, or even his guru, Shiv Brat Lal. Comments Faqir:

"O'Dayal's mother, whom you see within and whom you love within is your own creation, your own child. You, yourself, create the image of Shiv Brat Lal in your center of Trikuti, while other devotees create ideals such as Krishna, Rama, or other Gods at the same center and enjoy their vision. Man is basically ignorant about the reality. Mother Bhagyawati is not a lonely example. I too suffered many hardships due to his very ignorance." [9]

Faqir's insights, interestingly, tally with Book One of the *Tibetan Book of the Dead*. As Evans-Wentz comments:

"These Deities [manifestations of various gods and goddess in the intermediate plane] are in ourselves. They are not something apart from us. . . In this esoteric sense, the Lotus Order of Deities represent the deified principles of the vocal functions of ourselves. . . ." [10]

In this new chapter in Faqir's spiritual quest, he began to develop a dispassion for anything which arose in his meditation -- be it delightful or wrathful. Instead Faqir began to query, "Who is it that sees the light? Who is it that hears the sound?" In other words, what is it that experiences this world and worlds beyond it? No doubt, Faqir reasoned, it is consciousness. But what is that? wondered Faqir. The answer would haunt Faqir for the rest of his life, for he realized that no matter what spiritual practices he may do he would never know. It was simply incomprehensible, a mystery without limitation. To Faqir the haunting aspect about this discovery was that no human being (not even avatars, saints, or gurus), he surmised, could possibly know. Indeed, it was this very unknowability which constituted man's enlightenment, or so Faqir intuited. Argues Faqir:

"I do not proclaim that whatever I say is correct or final. Whatever I say is the conclusion of my experience of life. Nature is unfathomable. No one has known it. A small germ in a body cannot know the whole body. Similarly (a) human being is like a small germ in a vast Creation. How can he claim to have known the entire creation? Those who say that they have known are wrong. No one can describe or even know the entire creation. Up to a certain extent to which man's mind has access, one can say something. But nobody can tell about the entire universe. It is indescribable."

Paradoxically buoyed by this intuition, Faqir began to immerse himself more and more into the clear void light, forgetting himself and his quest in the process. Although Faqir's extraordinary excursions took place while he was still alive, and not in a near-death state, his experiences reinforce the general philosophy of the *Bardo Thotrol* about liberation.

"O Son of noble family, (name), listen. Now the pure luminosity of the dharmata is shining before you; recognize it. O son of noble family, at this moment your state of mind is by nature pure emptiness, it does not possess any nature whatever, neither substance or quality such as colour, but it is pure emptiness; this is the dharmata. . . This mind of yours is inseparable luminosity and emptiness in the form of a great mass of light, it has no birth or death, therefore it is the Buddha of Immortal Light. To recognize this is all that is necessary." [11]

What exactly this emptiness or luminosity is cannot, by definition, be described. In the *Tibetan Book of the Dead* the emphasis is on recognizing one's true nature, that which is no-thing in particular but rather the field in which all things arise -- itself being visionless, though producing visions; itself being structureless, though exhibiting structure; itself being non-existent, though producing existence. The clear void light is absolutely paradoxical, since the "I" cannot grasp it, nor can the mind by its subject/object dualism conceive it. Ken Wilber, a well regarded transpersonal theorist and practicing Zen Buddhist, describes it this way:

"The Absolute is both the highest state of being and the ground of being; it both the goal of evolution and the ground of evolution, the highest stage of development and the reality or suchness of all stages of development; the highest of all conditions and the Condition of all conditions; the highest rung in the ladder and the wood out of which the ladder is made. Anything less than that paradox generates either pantheistic reductionism, on the one hand, or wild and radical transcendentalism on the other. . . . " [12]

Thus Faqir, following his Tibetan counterparts, eschewed even the pure light and sound which was beyond form, and attached himself to no-thing, allowing himself, as he so astutely put it, to "hang on the gallows." But in so doing, Faqir broke with Radhasoami tradition, which advocates surat shabd yoga (lit., "uniting the soul with the divine inner sound"), and eventually became regarded as a "heretic." [13] Near the end of his life, Faqir grew closer to the philosophical principles of Buddhism, particularly Mahayana, as outlined in the *Bardo Thotrol*. Indeed, if one were only to look at his later writings, one would come away with the impression that Faqir came from a lineage of Tibetan lamas. The following passage is particularly relevant in this regard:

"O' Faqir these satsangis have taught you the method of hanging at the gallows. Only this experience of the manifestation of my form at different places, of which I am never aware, has changed my life. . . My experiences prove that Yogi, Meditator, Guru, Disciple and even the aspirant of salvation are in bondage. . . These people who create my form with their mental forces to fulfill their worldly desires are not interested to know the Truth. They do not hang themselves on the gallows, because they depend on the support of my Form. Whereas to a man on the gallows there is no support. This is the highest stage." [14]

It is precisely this letting go -- both of the objects which entice the mind and the mind itself -- which constitutes the final meditation in the *Tibetan Book of the Dead*. When this is done, no rebirth is possible, since there is no one left to reap experiences. But what happens to those who cannot let go into the clear void light? What is their plight? According to the *Bardo Thotrol*, such beings have a series of lesser options, whereby they can take new births in higher or lower dimensions of awareness. Regions upon regions exist where departed beings are enjoying the fruits of their karmic actions. Their fall, so to say, from the empty luminosity is due to one simple, but devastating mistake: they took the apparitions, the lights, the colors, the sounds, and the sensations of the intermediate plane to be real, and not as projections of their own self-created karma. In a phrase, they bought the dream as reality and were thus duped. Concerning these beings, the *Tibetan Book of the Dead* says:

"O son of noble family, if you do not recognize them [the various lights and apparitions] as your projections, whatever meditation practice you have done during your life, you have not met with this teaching, the coloured light will frighten you, the sounds will bewilder you and the rays of light will terrify you. If you do not understand this essential point of the teachings you will not the recognize the sounds, lights and rays, and so you will wander in samsara." [15]

Faqir Chand also reiterates the teachings of the *Bardo Thotrol* on this issue of karmic propensities (the principle that karma sways one away from the clear void light at death, if one is not attached beforehand in the empty luminosity). Faqir's frank autobiographical admissions reveal that even a sage as steeped in meditation as he could occasionally fall from the truth and get caught in the whirlpool of attachment. For instance, when Faqir Chand went to sleep he usually attached himself to the light and sound within, but occasionally would get caught up with dreams, falsely believing that he was seeing his father, his son, his wife, trains, and so on. As Faqir points out:

"This night I had a dream in which I saw running trains. An accident occurred; I carried my luggage; my father (whom I was afraid of) met me ahead. Then I met my mother; my first wife was also sitting there. I inquired from my wife, "What about your wounded leg? Is your leg now alright? Are you not my wife?" Meanwhile I awoke and attuned my Self to the Shabd (Inner Sound Current). . . All these deeds, thoughts and feelings where selfish motives are involved shall positively have their reaction upon the individual concerned, either in the waking state or in sleep. Why do I say so? This is my experience. Ever since the establishment of Manavta Mandir I have never dreamed about it. Why? Because my Self is neither attached to Mandir nor to any of you. But why do my father, mother, wife and railway trains appear time and again in my dreams? Because my Self was attached to them." [16]

Faqir's observation of what occurs in the dream state also holds true for what happens in the intermediate plane after death, since both involve the same fundamental rule: attachment creates repetition and thus the cycle of samsara continues. Liberation, both in the *Tibetan Book of the Dead* and in The *Unknowing Sage,* is non-attachment to anything or anyone. Only then can the bubble or knot of self-existence be undone.

When Faqir Chand was asked what would happen to him after death, he frankly remarked, "I don't know." When asked to elaborate, he proceeded to give a gist of his entire philosophy of life; not surprisingly, as I have attempted to point out in this paper, Faqir's outlook echoes almost point by point The *Tibetan Book of the Dead*:

"So what I have understood about Nam is that it is the true knowledge of the feelings, visions, and images that are seen within. This knowledge is that all the creations of the waking, dreaming and deep sleep modes of consciousness are nothing but samskaras (impressions which are in truth unreal) that are produced by the mind. What to speak about others, even I am not aware of my own Self (in dreams). Who knows what may happen to me at the time of death? I may enter the state of unconsciousness, enter the state of dreams and see railway trains. . . How can I make a claim about my attainment of the Ultimate? The truth is that I know nothing." [17]

Evans-Wentz, writing some forty years earlier than Faqir, makes the following observation concerning the *Bardo Thotrol*:

"It is not necessary to suppose that all the dead in the Intermediate State experience the same phenomena, any more than all the living do in the human world, or in dreams. . . As a man is taught, so he believes. . . . " [18]

In the end, Faqir's death was an untypical one. In April of 1981 he installed his spiritual successor, Dr. I.C. Sharma, at Manavta Mandir, Hoshiarpur, and then proceeded to fly to Pittsburgh, Pennsylvania, in the United States to conduct his fifth world tour. He was ninety-five years old. But just prior to departing from the Delhi airport, Faqir was asked in a tape-recorded meeting by a long-time friend and devotee when he would be coming back. Faqir, in an unusually prophetic reply, responded: "When I come back, it will be in black box." And so it was. Several weeks later in a Pittsburgh hospital Faqir after undergoing a cardiac arrest and suffering in a coma for several days died. [19] Days later his body was sent back to India in a casket for final cremation rights.

One can only wonder if the unknowing sage melted into the empty luminosity or into the dream world of running trains.

NOTES

[1] I will be using two translations here for my article: Evans-Wentz's famous work, The *Tibetan Book of the Dead* (New York: Causeway Books, 1973); and Francesca Mantle's and Chogyam Trungpa's The *Tibetan Book of the Dead* (Berkeley: Shambhala, 1975).

[2] Op. cit., pages 32 -33.

[3] Op. cit., page 4

[4] Op. cit., page 22.

[5] For more on the Radhasoami tradition, see Radha Swami Teachings by Lekh Raj Puri (Beas: Radha Soami Foundation, 1967).

[6] Op. cit., page 26. Also see Lane's "The Himalayan Connection" (*Journal of Humanistic Psychology*, Fall 1984) for more on the psychological implications of Faqir's visionary experiences.

[7] Op. cit., page 26. It should be pointed out that just prior to leaving to Iraq, Shiv Brat Lal informed Faqir that the ultimate guru was within one's self, nowhere on the outside. In fact, during this meeting, Shiv Brat Lal appointed Faqir as his spiritual successor, blessing his disciple with the following words: "Faqir, you are yourself the Supreme Master of your time. Start delivering spiritual discourses to the seekers and initiate them into the path of Sant Mat. In due course of time, your own satsangis [followers] will prove to be your "True Guru," and it is through your experiences with them that the desired secret of Sant Mat will be revealed to you." [Op. cit., page 25.]

[8] Evans-Wentz, op. cit., page 66

[9] Op. cit., page 48.

[10] Evans-Wentz, op.cit.

[11] Evans-Wentz, op. cit.

[12] Ken Wilber, *Eye to Eye*, page 266.

[13] See *The Radhasoami Tradition* for more information.

[14] Op. cit., page 50.

[15] Freemantle el al, op. cit., page 41.

[16] Op. cit., page 45.

[17] Op. cit., page 47.

[18] Evans-Wentz, op. cit., page 33.

[19] For more on Faqir's death, please refer to I.C. Sharma's Hindi biography of Faqir Chand entitled *Sidha Satpurusha Faqir Baba*.

The Honest Guru

Reflections on Unknowingness

Honesty is a virtue that is hard to come by. Sure people claim to have it or at least aspire to it, yet very few of us can be totally frank about our lives, our motivations, our hidden desires. It is particularly difficult for those who are in positions of authority. Why? Because it is precisely when we have some social status, some social leverage, and some social mobility that we run the risk of hurting another's feelings. Is a mother totally honest to her child? Does she not lie or deceive on occasion to avoid hurting the feelings of her tiny beloved? Is a teacher completely forthcoming to his student? Does he not blind himself occasionally from the obvious drawbacks of his pupil? Naturally, we would all admit to lying or deceiving at one time or another. The problematic issue in this is where we draw the line between harmless social lying and damaging personal dishonesty. It is a difficult issue, no doubt, and one which each of us faces moment-to-moment, day-to-day, and year-to-year.

This brings us to that most remarkable of 20th century Indian mystics, the late Baba Faqir Chand. One would be hard pressed to find a guru as disarmingly open as Faqir, who, unlike most of his colleagues in the Punjab, had repeatedly confessed to his human failings and his intellectual limitations. And it is exactly Faqir's honesty that sets him apart from other spiritual leaders; it is also Faqir's honesty that raises the question of Truth. Could it be, as Faqir would have us believe by his own life and example, that no saint or guru or mystic--however enlightened, however revered, and however popular--truly knows the secret of human existence? For skeptics the answer is already self-evident: nobody does know, especially religious leaders who are more often than not caught in mythic or pre-rational modes of thinking. For believers in religious truth, Faqir's confessions may be viewed as revelatory or misguided.

But in both camps, Faqir's honesty will most likely not be an issue. There is a certain trustworthiness about Faqir's confessional attitude which automatically endears the reader. But perhaps it is more than that, perhaps deep within our own hearts and minds we intuit that Reality is indeed greater than we can conceive; that God--and I am using the term to denote Absoluteness--is not something to be talked about, or theorized about, or even proven. God is that which begins and ends in the Unknowable, and thus agnosticism is closer to our own bone than we might wish to admit. We really don't know, do we? Maybe what makes Faqir Chand 's confession of ignorance so appealing and so believable is that he is stating a universal fact-

-a fact which is evident to every human being who has ever lived: we simply don't know the why of our own existence, much less the reason behind the universe. And this unknowingness may not be a cultural product at all, but rather an inherent, even biological, response to the very wonder of the cosmos.

In any case, what we have in the writings of Faqir Chand is a unique autobiographical confession about the inner workings of a well-regarded mystic. What we have, in sum, is an honest guru. Although for Westerners the term "honest guru" may seem to be an oxymoron, in Faqir Chand the phrase is perfectly apt and attests to his distinctive style. How many gurus are there who say that they don't know what happens after death? Or that they may just be plain wrong in their observations? Or that they have no power whatsoever to perform miracles? Or that they suffer from the same weaknesses as other human beings? Certainly there may be some, but the number is exceptionally small. Moreover, out of this small circle very few have spoken with the clarity and conviction of Baba Faqir Chand.

To read Faqir is to read yourself; to end up where you started in the first place: not knowing. Not knowing may be undesirable, it may even be frightening, but it does have one immeasurable advantage to those who feel it, who contemplate it, and who don't resist it: it is a truthful and honest human response to the mystery of the universe. Faqir Chand, unlike most of humankind, dove daily into the very mystery of his being, and each time he emerged he came out with the same message: "I don't know." But instead of finding that discovery to be useless, he found it, along with Socrates, Lao Tzu and others, to be the greatest wisdom of all.

I have never seen two people fight over their "unknowingness"; however, I have seen wars fought and millions of humans exterminated over people claiming they "knew"--whether that knowledge be cloaked in the guise of Communism, Racism, or any host of isms. True knowledge is knowing that you don't know; true wisdom is knowing that nobody else does either. Faqir Chand can be regarded as an enlightened being in the sense that he came to grips with the Unknowable. Not by super-imposing order or meaning upon that Mystery, but rather by surrendering to its transformative implications: *Transcendental Unknowingness creates natural humility and an inherent openness to the vagaries of Being.*

FAQIR CHAND'S LETTER
Concerning His Autobiography

Dear David, I have gone through your letter. You can do this work. I will help you with all the experiences of my life, as how I started it, how I can in contact with my Spiritual Master. I will dictate it in Urdu and then the same after translating into English will be sent to you in about a month's time or so. I am an old man and unwell at the moment. I heartily wish you success in your life in all aspects.

Yours in Him,
Faqir

FAQIR CHAND'S LETTER
Concerning Meditation

Try to penetrate within yourself. Leave physical senses by repeating Holy Name given to you by your Guru without moving your tongue. Meditate on image of your Guru but if one thinks that his guru is a man, he cannot go above the mind. Concentrate on image is necessary for leaving the mental vibrations. Then comes light and Sound. Try to know what is that sees light within or listens Sounds within. That is THOU alone. Then one can realize who is HE: his search ends and becomes the same reality, My love . . .

FAQIR CHAND'S LETTER
Concerning Unknowing

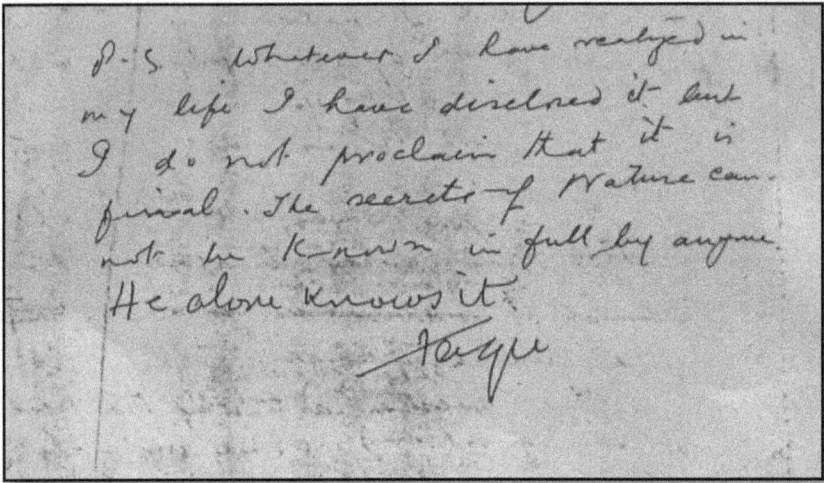

P.S. Whatever I have realized in my life I have disclosed it but I do not proclaim that it is final. The secrets of Nature cannot be known in full by anyone. He alone knows it.

--Faqir

FAQIR CHAND'S LETTER
Concerning Meditation

Try to penetrate within yourself. Leave physical senses by repeating Holy Name given to you by your Guru without moving your tongue. Meditate on image of your Guru but if one thinks that his guru is a man, he cannot go above the mind. Concentrate on image is necessary for leaving the mental vibrations. Then comes light and Sound. Try to know what is that sees light within or listens Sounds within. That is THOU alone. Then one can realize who is HE: his search ends and becomes the same reality, My love . . .

FAQIR CHAND'S LETTER
Concerning Unknowing

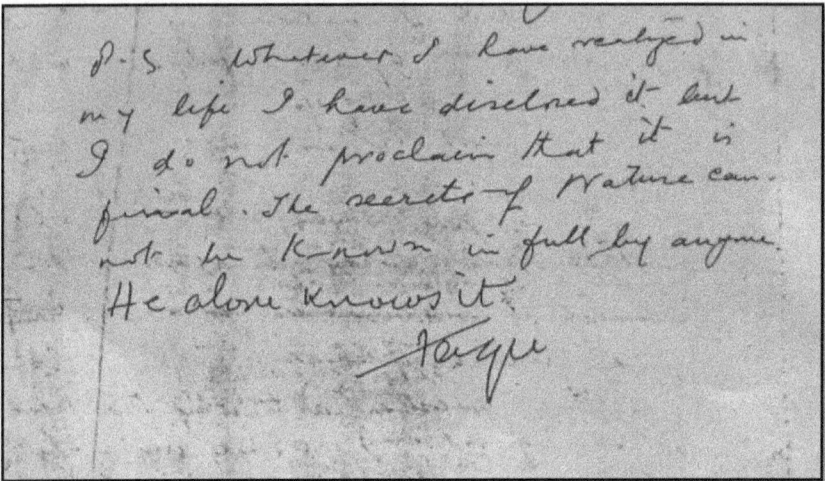

P.S. Whatever I have realized in my life I have disclosed it but I do not proclaim that it is final. The secrets of Nature cannot be known in full by anyone. He alone knows it.

--Faqir

Select Bibliography

Books and Pamphlets by Baba Faqir Chand. All texts are available for free online as PDFs at the Manavta Mandir website.

A Broadcast On Reality

A Word to Americans

A Word to Canadians

Autobiography Of Faqir

Divine Message On Self Realisation

Jeevan Mukti

Message On Independence Day

Know Thyself to Know God

Manavta Manavta

The True Religion

The Essence of Truth

Republic Day Message

Nam-Dan

Satya Sanatan Dharam

The Art of Happy Living

The Secret of Secrets

Weight of Soul

Yogic philosophy of Saints

The Master Speak to the Foreigners

Truth Always Wins

Recommended Readings:

My personal three favorites of Faqir Chand's English books are: 1) *Jeevan Mukti*; 2) *The Secret of Secrets*; and 3) *The Essence of Truth*. These are essentially transcripts (sometimes verbatim) from Faqir Chand's satsangs over the years at Manavta Mandir at elsewhere. Professor Bhagat Ram Kamal's translations are very clear and lucid and convey Faqir's message without ambiguity. It should also be kept in mind that Faqir's later writings are more confessional and forthcoming about his unknowingness and thus each book should be read in context and in light of Faqir's increasing age.

For Further Information:

Manavta Mandir, Sutheri Road, Hoshiarpur, Punjab, India